SUCKED DRY

The Struggle is Reel

CHARLIE LEVINE

ISBN-13: 978-0-9985438-2-6
ISBN: 0-9985438-2-9

TABLE OF CONTENTS

To Diane, the compass that guides me through every storm.

CHAPTER ONE

Miles and Miles

You ungrateful son of a bitch! I have been nothing but a dedicated, indentured servant, safely taking you through miles and miles of sun-drenched waterfront, and you, you wanton, show no thanks and no gratitude.

Every day you slip me under your sole, step into my comfort zone, use me and abuse me.

I can feel it when you pivot on your balls, pushing all of your weight into the soft beds that I've provided. I can feel you grinding sea salt and sand deep within me. I can feel those trickles of pee that bounce off your knee and dribble down on top of me.

Some days I hate you. Parker, can you hear me? I hate you!

My worst day started off as one of my best. We stood together on the bow of a Costa Rican skiff, fishing the rocks off the tip of the Osa Peninsula. You threw that fly like a savant, casting the flashy bucktail into the rocky surf.

You stood on me and I supported you through every back cast, every double haul and every perfect presentation of the fly that sliced through the heaving surf. I never let go of my grip on the pitching fiberglass deck, even when the bow sunk and crashed into the swells. I helped you. I held you in place, Parker! You didn't fall. You kept casting and it paid off, dear brother. It paid off!

Finally, the erect dorsal comb of a roosterfish pierced the green water as the head of a 50-pound marauder pushed up a wake behind the fly. I bet you didn't even think of me as you stripped that line faster, faster.

Did you once remember me as you put all of your weight behind that strip set? I bet you would've if you'd fallen. I would've taken the fall. You are a true son of a bitch!

What if I had given up and let you slide off that boat? But no, never! I stuck to that fiberglass casting deck like a hammered nail throughout the entire battle. I couldn't let you down. I'm here to keep you on your toes, so to speak.

You ran around the deck of that little boat, retrieving line, swinging the rod tip in all directions to keep tight to that gorgeous animal. It was an honor to serve you in that regard, my dear sir. I too felt the triumph as you brought the game fish beside the boat. I felt your pulse race as the fish's striped flanks flashed brightly through the clear, green water. I was part of that battle.

But that night, Parker ... what you did to me ... what I saw.

The sticky floors of those cantinas. The gurry of the fish slime you left on me. The bathroom with the grayish, ankle-deep mystery liquid that you tiptoed through. And now, now that we're out in public and amid all of these pedestrians, I feel ugly and barbaric. I'm stained. Wrought with memories of remarkable fish fights and long, bar-strewn nights. At least you showered. I stink, Parker! I stink like a dried pogie in the sun. I'm a warrior, a victor, yet I smell like a piece of dung stuck to a cow's tail. How could you treat me so unfairly?

The stewardess tapped me on the shoulder, interrupting the music I had blaring in my headphones.

"Sir, I'm going to have to ask you to remove your sandals," she said.

"I'm sorry ... what?"

She pointed to my feet, then moved her hand up to her nose and squeezed her nostrils.

"There have been complaints from the other passengers," she said.

I looked around and noticed that everyone sitting near me had managed to shift themselves to the farthest corners of their seats. Each person was trying to flee but was trapped by the confines of their narrow, imitation-leather chairs.

I looked up at the stewardess. Sorry, flight attendant.

"They're not that bad," I said, removing my left flip-flop. The sandal made a squelching noise as I pulled it from my skin. It sounded like a bare, hot, sticky human thigh freeing itself from a vinyl, cooler-top cushion.

Once removed, I noticed the tan lines on the top of my foot. I had a bright-white, upside-down, V-shaped mark, and a little black gunk in the notch between my big toe and second toe.

The people around me watched in terror as I held the loose flop in my hand. I bet I could've hijacked the plane with nothing more than my sandal. People wanted to run, but they were trapped. Nowhere to go. Nowhere to hide.

One old lady reached up, trying desperately to crank the circular air vent above her to the most free-flowing position it offered. She longed to breathe in that good, good recirculated air.

I slowly moved the flip-flop to my nose. The stewardess leaned back against the seat behind her trying to get away from it. I took a sniff, my nostrils just inches from the black, tar-like sole of the sandal. Fear and dread whooshed through the fuselage.

"They're not that bad," I said again.

She made a face of pure disgust — her freckled nose crinkled like a piece of beef jerky, her lips pierced tightly, the edges turning white from the pressure. Her eyes got tight, no larger than a pair of dimes as she tried to burn a hole through my skull with her hateful stare and incinerate me, right there in 23C.

She stormed away and returned in a flash wearing rubber gloves and holding a Ziploc freezer bag.

"Surrender the shoes!" she demanded.

"Having me sit here barefoot is not going to help the situation," I said. "Seriously, is this how you treat someone who's incontinent and just shit their pants? You embarrass them in front of the rest of the passengers? What kind of airline is this? Maybe I have a foot disorder!"

I couldn't get the last line out without cracking a smile.

She held the bag open.

"I will get you some footwear," she said.

"OK, fine," I said. "And a drink, please. Captain Morgan and Coke."

"Deal," she said.

I acquiesced, handing over my old, trusty pair of stinky sandals. As I gave her the rank shoes, I thought of all the fish I had caught in them. The miles of beaches we'd walked. The rum bars we'd scampered through. Then, the gorgonzola smell wafted up and struck me hard. I cleared my throat.

It's just as well, I thought.

She zipped the sandals tightly in the plastic bag and held it with two fingers as if the thin layer of clear plastic was the only protection between her and an infectious disease that might overtake her.

She walked down the aisle to the galley and came back with a pair of slippers from first class. White, terrycloth and pretty comfy.

I leaned over and made eye contact with the old bag breathing through her hands next to me.

"How do they look?" I asked.

My name is Parker McPhee. I love to fish. These are my stories.

CHAPTER TWO

First Light

I would've never known my father, I mean really known him, had it not been for the time we spent fishing together. Many people relied on Joe McPhee. He was torn in a million different directions. He was the heart, the epicenter, of many worlds. His businesses needed him, his colleagues needed him, his customers needed him, his lady friends needed him, and then there was me. I needed him too. But the only times I truly had him all to myself were the days and nights we spent fishing together.

The most cherished days of my youth were spent alongside Daddy's hulking frame, trolling around Long Island Sound, him driving the boat with his feet on the steering wheel as he leaned back in the captain's chair. He preferred to take his shirt off as soon as the summer season allowed so he could feel the warmth of the sun on his skin. He kept himself in shape and wasn't afraid to show off a bit. If he wasn't working or in a meeting, he was doing something physical. Restoring old cars, helping out on the shop floor or tending to his small armada of boats.

Daddy's hands were not the typical soft-as-a-chinchilla hands you'd expect from a businessman. His were strong from turning wrenches, calloused from lifting weights and cracked from cold mornings spent sitting in a duck blind or casting plugs. The salt and sun tanned his skin. He never wore sunblock, but few did in those days. He liked the way a sunburn felt on his face. It meant he was doing something that he loved to do. That something could be splitting wood in the backyard or running through Plum Gut on his way to Montauk, the last bit of civilization on the tip of Long Island, New York, which served as his stopping-off point before motoring on toward the continental shelf in search of the giant game fish found in the deep, offshore canyons.

Most of the people Daddy did business with kept golf clubs in the trunks of their luxury sedans, but not my father. He hated golf.

Found it infuriating. So many hours devoted to hitting a little ball into a little hole. Daddy filled his vehicles with an ever-changing mishmash of coolers, foul-weather gear, fishing rods, marine electronics, alpine skis and shotguns, depending on the time of year. He was always ready for an adventure. And there was always a woman around whom he could scoop up and bring along on the boat or to some deer stand in the woods.

He once shot a duck while getting a blowjob in his favorite duck blind on some quiet marsh in eastern Long Island. He never gave her a warning. His neck was angled perfectly to spot the ducks coming in. He was rather enjoying himself and didn't want to tell the young lady to stop, so he just reached for his gun, took aim and blasted away while she was on her knees. He's lucky she didn't bite his dick off when he fired his over/under 20-gauge just a few inches from her head.

"It was the perfect shot," I overheard him say to one of his buddies. He told that story a lot. Daddy had many conquests, but there was only one woman who took his heart.

My mother passed away when I was three and I have very few memories of her. She was a slight blond woman with crystal-blue eyes that I was lucky enough to inherit. Her name was Maggie. Everyone who knew her speaks of her zest for life, love of nature, wit and precise comedic timing. She always had a snippy retort to Daddy's jokes and innuendo. They laughed endlessly, until the diagnosis.

It all happened so quickly. While skiing in Vermont she became dizzy to the point of losing her ability to walk. She went to the hospital. They took some X-rays and diagnosed her with inoperable brain cancer. Her funeral was a short eight weeks later.

After her death, Daddy went rogue. He hired nannies to care for me and did his thing, working ridiculous hours. His top priority became growing the business. Second was fishing. His personal projects, cars and boats followed. I think he kind of forgot about me. I was so young and found myself connecting to my nannies and the various people who worked around the house to fill the void. I don't remember much from this time, to be honest.

As I got older I was sent to counseling. The therapists loved to tell me that I had not only lost my mother, but in many ways, I'd lost my father too. According to the guy holding the pad, Daddy preferred to stay busy as a way to avoid grieving.

Women were drawn to Daddy. He had strong, dark features. Ink-black hair as thick as a rug, broad shoulders and a vibrant smile with perfect teeth. He never married after my mother passed. He was just 31 when it happened, but he could never bring himself to love again. Not like that. So he just played around, and worked. And when he wasn't working, he fished or went hunting.

My mother was a waitress at a small, family-owned diner in New Rochelle, New York, when she met Daddy, who was traveling through visiting accounts.

"I walked into that diner exhausted," Daddy told me. "It was one of those brutal days. I think I had five or six sales meetings and I was totally spent. Dog-tired. I saw this diner and figured I'd get some coffee and maybe some eggs. So I stumble into the place and sit in a booth by the window. I was looking out the window at nothing much. New Rochelle isn't exactly Venice. I was just zoning out when your mother sat down in the booth with me, right across the table, smiling. When I saw her, I was speechless. It was unlike anything I'd ever felt, Parker. My skin dimpled with goosebumps but I tried to play it cool. I didn't even realize she was the waitress."

"What did you say, Daddy?"

"I didn't say anything. We just stared at each other for a little while, smiling oddly, and then she asked, 'For here or to go?' And I said, 'That depends.' I watched her eyes going back and forth as she looked into my left eye and then my right, like she was trying to tell if I was a bullshitter or something. Then she says, 'Depends on what?' And that's when I had the best line of my life: 'Whether or not you're coming with me.'"

I rolled my eyes. It sounded so corny to my prepubescent ears.

"That really worked?"

"She laughed, and she had a great laugh. It was deep and her cheeks would go red and her eyes would fill up with happy tears. That woman loved to laugh, Parker, and it would infect everybody

11

around her. She just radiated joy."

Things moved pretty quickly after that. Daddy found reasons to visit New Rochelle on a regular basis and they began to date. He met her parents, and in eight months, they were living together back in Connecticut. Daddy was in his late twenties, and my mother was 21. When Daddy knocked her up, they eloped to New Hampshire. After I came along, she never went anywhere without me. In the three short years I had with her, there was never a day we were apart. At least that's what Daddy told me. My only real memory of her was going to the beach and building sand castles. Sometimes I have dreams of this blond, curly-haired woman with eyes the color of the Caribbean Sea. I'm pretty sure it's her.

As Daddy threw himself into work, days and weeks would pass with barely a few glimpses of him. I'd see him for dinner some nights, but on many evenings his secretary would call the house to say he had to work late or travel. It was painful to spend so much time alone at a young age. But every time I was about to blow up on him for being so distant, he'd appear.

"Hey Parker, how about we sneak away for the weekend," he'd say. The loveliest words I'd ever heard. He'd pick me up at school on a Friday wearing his olive-colored deck boots. His blue Ford Bronco would be packed to the gills with mountains of tackle, food, ropes, anchors, harpoons, you name it. Daddy never forgot anything when it came to gear.

I loved those drives down to the boat, chatting about the trip we were going to embark on. He'd tell me about the areas we were headed to, Montauk or Block Island, how long it would take to get there, where our course would take us, and the types of fish we were targeting. He kept the boat in Old Saybrook, Connecticut, at the mouth of the Connecticut River and within a two- or three-hour run to Block Island, depending on the tides.

Each summer, from the time I was four or five, Daddy would take me on a handful of fishing trips, usually just the two of us. Sometimes he'd let me bring a friend, but I preferred to be alone with him. We would fish long days on his boat, targeting summer flounder around Block or striped bass and bluefish around Montauk. In the evening we would tie up, head into town and go out for dinner. By 10 o'clock, my young body was cooked. I'd crawl into my sleeping bag and sack out in one of the boat's single berths. The clang of halyards on nearby sailboats slapping against the mast would lull me into a deep sleep. I often went to bed with crusty hair from salt spray and the smell of bait on my hands. The boat shower never worked that well. Sometimes I'd rinse the salt off with a freshwater hose or hit the marina showers. But I didn't mind the scratch of salt on my skin.

Daddy would lie down on the V-berth in the bow with a book. He slept lightly and would bounce out of bed if anything odd happened. Sometimes the anchor would drag in the harbor. Or the wind would increase overnight and he'd have to adjust the lines if we were tied up at a marina. I remember a bilge alarm going off once. Millions of things can pull you out of sleep on a boat and Daddy was ready for just about any of them.

Sometimes he fired up the motors early and we'd leave the dock before I awoke. When my eyes opened and I peered out of the porthole in my bunk, all I saw was moving water. We were under way. That's the best way to wake up.

The droll of the single diesel engine always calmed Daddy's nerves as we trolled along at a steady clip of six or seven knots, just fast enough for our lures to mimic the menhaden that our core target, the striped bass, was after.

We'd troll the deep-water edges of The Race, a rocky stretch of bottom where Long Island Sound meets Block Island Sound and the deeper waters of the Atlantic Ocean. The currents pushed and pulled over the rocky ledges, trapping bait, making it easy for the big bass and bluefish to snack on them.

"I'm marking bait on the bottom, Parker," he'd say from the helm. "Drop a diamond jig down there."

With my thumb over the spool, I let the jig sink until it hit bottom and the line went slack. I engaged the reel, took three quick cranks on the handle to get the lure up out of the rocks, and started bouncing it, making large sweeps with my fishing rod. The shine of the jig and the white bucktail tied on the hook drew the bass like hungry mosquitoes. Not even five feet tall and hanging onto a fishing rod with all of my strength. More than once the fish would take me to the rail and pin me against the side of the boat. Daddy'd just laugh. He loved it.

"That's your fish," he'd say. "If you give me the rod, it becomes mine."

Never.

Determination often prevailed, but sometimes he stepped in.

"Maybe you're hung up on the bottom," he'd say, knowing full well there was a 40-pounder down there, whipping its giant mouth around like a windsock. "Let me see if I can't get you out of there."

He'd take the rod, get the fish's head turned so it'd start coming up toward the surface and hand the rod back to let me finish the fight. It took me years to figure out his little tricks.

"Nice fish, Parker!" he'd yell as the big bass finally appeared next to the boat. Daddy grabbed the fish's mouth with his rough thumb, hoisting the animal out of the water with his bare hands. I knew that once Daddy got his hands on a fish the animal wouldn't get away. I couldn't keep a big fish in my young mitts. It'd flop right out of my grip like a tree frog. Daddy's strength inspired me and made me feel safe.

He'd take my photo with a 35mm camera he kept on the boat. I would kneel on the deck to pose with the fish because these bass were too big for me to lift. We released nearly all of our striped bass, a foreign idea to most crews at the time, but Daddy wasn't out to kill anything more than what we could eat. He told me that striped bass were being annihilated faster than they could reproduce, and he was right. At one point the government had to put a moratorium on the fish, making it illegal for anyone to kill a striped bass. It was the only way to save them. It worked. And in doing so, taught thousands of anglers the importance of conservation.

Our trips together took place long before the advent of cell phones. There was only the VHF radio should an emergency arise or you need to reach out and bug someone. On more than one occasion Daddy would call a marine operator to patch him through to some conference call, but the interruptions were limited then. Not like today. We weren't tweeting, beeping and vibrating. We enjoyed the sound of the ocean, gulls squawking and the wind whistling.

We'd spend hours talking.

"Have I ever told you how I used to play rugby?" he asked me once.

"No, I don't think so."

"I really wasn't any good, but I was big for my age. All the kids I hated, the over-privileged assholes, played rugby so I decided to give it a shot. It was the only way I could legally smack those fuckers in the mouth," he said with a big grin.

He told me about being a boy, fishing for yellow perch with his Uncle Sam.

"Much of what I learned about being a man started with fishing," he said. "My uncle didn't really know much about fishing, but he'd take me because I kept pestering him. I would lose fish because I couldn't tie a knot. I got a book about fishing from the library and learned every knot in it. I didn't know anything then, so I made it my goal to learn something new every time I went fishing. I took that same tactic in business and in life, really. I always asked a lot of questions and found guys who were better than me so I could learn from them. And it has served me well."

Daddy christened his first boat *Long Gone* because to him the ocean represented a great unknowingness, a place you could hide. That's what he wanted — to be adrift and out of reach — if only for a day or two. Obscured by the fog and cloaked by the swells.

He used the *Long Gone* name on subsequent boats but never placed Roman numerals next to the name to indicate he was on his fourth of fifth boat. He wasn't out to impress anyone. He just wanted to go fishing.

By the time I was 12, Daddy was on his third *Long Gone*, a 36-foot Downeast-style lobster boat. It was the first boat he had custom-built to his specifications, and though he went on to earn enough money to easily purchase a vessel two or three times the size of *Long Gone*, Daddy never did. He liked her as she was. He felt confident in her, and he could easily manage the boat on his own. She wasn't the biggest boat on the dock nor was she the prettiest, but to me, she represented everything right with the world. She had soft curves and a sharp entry on the bow. The hull was not a planing hull; it displaced the water for a soft, albeit rather slow ride. She'd pitch and roll in the waves but never left us adrift in some of the worst weather the North Atlantic threw at us. And with only one diesel engine, she sipped on fuel sparingly so we could make far runs to the offshore canyons.

Daddy had an infatuation with bluefin tuna, and these beasts taxed a crew to its core. Strong as an elephant and as fast as a Fiat, the bluefin tuna was the ultimate challenge for a Northeast fisherman. Each year the run of giants varied. Some years the fish would follow schools of herring right along the shores of Cape Cod. Other years they were found far offshore of Nantucket, way out in the shipping lanes. Daddy would move *Long Gone* depending on how the tuna migrated. Most years, he'd start bluefin season in Point Judith, Rhode Island. From there he'd fish Hudson Canyon or move north to Cape Cod. We docked in Hyannis, Massachusetts, located at the beginning of the Cape's elbow. From this location, he could either steer her north through the Cape Cod Canal to fish Stellwagen Bank, or run south of Nantucket to target Hydrographer's or one of the other long-range canyons beyond the continental shelf.

Daddy kept the boat fueled and loaded with tackle that was up to the task. Bluefin will bust your hooks, smoke your reels and make mincemeat of your heaviest line. Daddy carried triplicates of everything, from pliers to fuel filters. *Long Gone* had a custom tuna tower that stretched high above the enclosed helm station. It was the tallest tower the builder said our boat could take. From this vantage point, a good 18 feet off the surface of the ocean, Daddy could spot the giant predators as they motored across the waves. The giants may travel in small schools of just a few fish or larger pods of 50 or more. He used massive reels loaded with line that wouldn't snap under the extreme pressure of an 800-plus-pound giant tuna — reels built to carry enough 130-pound test line to give the angler a fighting chance. Daddy sent the reels to California to a special shop that could machine the drag systems to utilize every bit of pressure possible to put the brakes to these giants of the sea. It was manly shit.

The invites to chase bluefin with Daddy were not to be taken lightly. This wasn't amateur hour. It was the real deal. If you got in the way or required babysitting, you weren't asked back. Daddy would often go offshore alone, locating, hooking and battling the giants all by himself.

Reeling in a tuna over 500 pounds is akin to climbing a mountain with a truck tire tied to your waist. You gain a few steps and then the tire pulls you back down. There is constant pressure. Something is always pulling. You or the fish, and more often it's the fish.

"The biggest tuna I ever caught weighed almost 900 pounds," Daddy told me one night as we sat together at the helm of *Long Gone*. "I was all by myself too."

I shook my head in disbelief: "How?"

"It was one of those incredible years. The Gulf Stream had pushed in close to the canyons and I had the boat in Point Judith. It was a last-minute thing and I just decided to go out alone. I had hooked and lost a big fish earlier in the week so I was itching to get back out there. I caught some live bluefish and a couple of Boston mackerel on the way to the fishing grounds and I had them in the bait tank. After I lost that big fish I had a couple of guys in the shop take an empty steel drum and weld some eyelets along the top of it. This was going to be my impenetrable harpoon ball, but it didn't really work out that way.

"I hooked up maybe 40 miles south of Block Island. I was drifting with just one bait down 50 feet. I marked some fish at 200 feet and ran over to the rod and threw it into free-spool. I dropped the bait down. The tuna hit the bait on the drop, and I have no idea how I kept the reel from backlashing into a giant bird's nest."

"How'd you know it was a tuna?" I asked.

"Because the spool went from a slow steady speed on the drop to a fucking tornado. It was like I had dropped a baseball off the Empire State Building! I engaged the drag and set the hook. The fish damn near spooled me, Parker. Took a mile of line in a few seconds. I was lucky I didn't have the boat on the anchor; I would've been screwed. I was able to start her up and go after the fish."

"But you need to reel in the line as you go after the fish, right?"

17

He nodded emphatically, his teeth showing through a wide smile. "Oh yeah. I had one hand on the wheel and would let go of it and crank on the reel like a crazy person every chance I got. I reeled in maybe half of the line, but then the fish sounded deep, just torpedoed for the bottom. There was no way I could slow it down without breaking the line."

"So, what did you do?"

"I'll tell you, but you're not going to believe me."

"Tell me, Daddy!"

"I attached the rod to the steel barrel with a super-heavy-duty snap swivel and kicked the whole thing over the side. Rod, reel, fish, everything. Just threw it all into the water."

He was laughing. I laughed too.

"You're like Quint!" I said, referring to the deranged captain from *Jaws*.

"I followed the barrel around for a few miles until it stopped. Dragging that thing just wore the fish out, but I was afraid it may have ruined the fish's meat," he said.

A fish will build up lactic acid in its muscles as it fights against the pull of the fishing line. If the fish overheats, the meat can become mushy and less desirable. Daddy wanted to sell this bluefin, so he needed to catch it quickly to get the highest price per pound.

"What happened next?" I asked.

"I pulled the barrel back on board. I unsnapped the swivel and stuck the rod and reel in a rod holder. I started cranking in the big dead fish, which was no fucking easy chore either. I tried to plane the fish up with the boat, but I was all alone. It took me a good five hours to retrieve all of the line. To this day I can't believe a shark never came around and ate her off the hook.

"When I got the fish to the boat, I struggled to get a tail rope around her because I had one hand on the fishing line, but I did it. And then I just collapsed on the deck. I was so spent."

He pulled the fish's tail in through the tuna door of the transom and tied it off. Then he reached over the transom with a fillet knife and made a cut in between the gills to let the blood run out of the fish and started motoring home.

"Is that the big tuna tail you have at the hunting cabin?" I asked.

He nodded: "It reminds me never to be scared to go after it alone."

The end game in big-game fishing is always the hardest part. By the time you manage to winch a giant fish to the boat, your body is completely wasted. Hands cramped. Back burning. We had a gin-pole on *Long Gone*, which used a block and tackle made up of a rope and a series of pulleys to hoist the fish up in the air by its tail and swing it onto the deck. But even after you get a fish into the boat, the work is still far from over. You have to clean a bluefin tuna immediately. If you don't care for the fish, the meat will lose its integrity.

Cleaning a giant tuna is a blood bath. You begin by taking a hand saw to the gill plate, sawing across the fish's hard armor to expose the gill rakers. The gill plate on a 600-pound tuna is the size of a large serving platter. With the gill removed, you sever the innards by the fish's anal vent (aka the asshole). Then you head back to the head and begin yanking out all of the guts. Daddy loved it. He'd reach in with both hands and throw handfuls of intestines and organs over the side of the boat. If the fish weighed more than 600 pounds, Daddy's arms couldn't reach deep enough into the cavity to remove everything. He'd use a hose and wash out the inside of the animal as best he could, then begin stuffing the void with ice. The stuffed bluefin core was zipped into a massive cooler bag and secured on deck for the long ride home.

On a good season Daddy would catch five or six big fish, but I think he felt privileged to catch just one. With his work schedule being what it was back then, I'm amazed he even found the time. He made time, I suppose.

Daddy's riches were built on sweat. He dug in with all his might and never let go. He never attended college and barely finished high school. He began working in a machine shop at a young age, running presses and welding. He started his own little shop when he was 25, after six years as an apprentice. With little interest in getting married or settling down, he just worked. And worked. And worked.

By the time he was 30, he held patents on machine systems that produced 12 different types of coils and springs. His machines produced coils for products as small as hearing aids all the way up to the 20-foot springs used in the suspension systems of massive, earth-moving machines with tires taller than most homes.

He grew his business, International Coil and Spring, into a $100 million enterprise. He sent products across the country and abroad, and maintained a staff of more than 200 employees.

Some people are addicted to drugs; others favor sex. Daddy's affliction was growing his business. He grew up poor. His mother was an alcoholic who failed pretty miserably at child rearing. Daddy never knew his own father, and it weighed on him his entire life. My grandmother couldn't manage her own life, let alone raise Daddy. He ended up staying with his Aunt Dorothy and her husband, Sam. They rescued Daddy from his mom and brought him up as best they could. Sam was a union electrician who never said too much, and Dorothy worked as a librarian in the town library. It was Sam who bought Daddy his first fishing pole.

Daddy always said that fishing was the only way he could erase his mind. He was good at fishing too. And he needed that success in his life. His childhood was far from easy. His mother kept the local bars in business and had a long list of suitors. There was some doubt as to who his father even was. The neglect made Daddy a bit of a loaner. He had no brothers or sisters. Fishing was the escape he needed when his mother came home fall-down drunk or yelled at him for no apparent reason. Fishing was also a way for Daddy to put food in his stomach.

Uncle Sam and Daddy would bring their cane poles to the local ponds and reservoirs throughout southern Connecticut. Daddy would dig up worms for bait or use crickets if he could catch them. Sam taught him how to tie on a hook and use a bobber or a cork as best he could, but he wasn't much of a fisherman. Daddy caught bass from the ponds and trout from the streams. Whenever he had money he'd go to the hardware store and buy new hooks, fishing line and a lure. And whenever his birthday came around, Sam would add some more gear to Daddy's tackle box. Eventually Sam and Daddy made their way to the shoreline, and the world of saltwater angling came into focus. Once Daddy caught his first saltwater fish, a baby bluefish called a snapper blue, he pretty much forgot about the palm-size trout he'd been landing in the neighborhood streams.

Daddy went to the beach every chance he got. He'd take the train and then a bus — fishing rod and tackle box in tow — then walk a couple of miles to reach the public beach in West Haven. He'd set up early and stay till dark, fishing with chunk bait and casting plugs. He'd watch the boats come and go from the harbor entrance, wondering where they might be coming from or where they were going. The idea of fishing offshore was only a dream then. He wanted nothing more than to stand on a boat and cruise off into the distance. He wondered what creatures he'd encounter out there in the deepness of the ocean. Those dreams became an unquenchable desire to own his own boat someday and go fishing whenever he wanted. A simple-sounding goal that's not so easy to attain.

"I fell in love with the ocean," Daddy said. "It never discriminates. You can be a rich man or a poor man and it'll treat you just the same."

I attended boarding schools and saw less and less of him as I began to sprout hair under my arms. I longed for summer days on the boat, but those trips had dried up almost entirely by the time I became a teenager. I communicated with him mostly through the headmaster's office by getting in trouble. Firecrackers in the hallways, practical jokes with dead fish, busted windows and BB guns. I smoked some grass here and there. Kid stuff. But it annoyed the hell out of him to have to leave a meeting to get me out of whatever mischief I found myself in. He missed most of my sporting events, and holidays were usually spent at a restaurant or company gathering. We were losing one another; the hook was

---

about to pull.

When I was 22 and finishing my junior year of college in St. Petersburg, Florida, Daddy called for me. He was in the hospital with an illness that he couldn't shake. I hung up the phone in disbelief, or denial. He'd never been sick. I couldn't remember him ever spending a day in bed.

The doctors diagnosed him with liver disease, and he was failing rapidly. I left school to go home to Connecticut to see him. It was the longest plane ride of my life. The questions swirled around in my head like a tropical storm. How bad was all this? Why didn't he call me sooner?

Walking into that hospital room, I spotted a man who was literally half the size of my father. His once broad shoulders and thick barrel chest were gone. His body was bony. He must've lost 45 pounds since I last saw him. His skin was noticeably jaundiced. Yellowed like the ceiling of a smoky bar. His hands were shaky and I could see the outline of his bones through the skin, which hung on him like a shroud.

I always admired my father's hands. Strong, manly hands. Hands that could change a transmission and lay a firm handshake on someone. These were not Daddy's hands.

"Here," he said, motioning to a corner of his bed when I stepped closer. "Parker, sit with me."

I sat down, holding back my tears and shock.

"You sure are handsome," he said, smiling. "A little bit of your Daddy in your eyes. I'm sure the ladies love you."

I half nodded. I was afraid to talk. The lump in my throat hurt. I wanted to cry so badly, but I was afraid my tears might destroy him even more than the liver disease.

"I want to tell you that I love you," he said. "I know I didn't do the best job raising you, but I tried. All those days we spent fishing ... I loved it. I hope you know that."

He spoke slowly. His face struggling to hold back the emotion. The whites of his strong, dark eyes had yellowed, his strength stolen from him. He was lying on his back and I don't think he could've sat up to hug me if he wanted to.

"Watching you grow up. I just ... I'm sorry for not spending more time with you, Parker. I got so caught up in work, and I wish I had made more time to do more with you."

I couldn't talk.

"You are my inspiration, you know," he said. "When I was young and fired up, I always thought of you. Of building a legacy for you. So, when you became a man, I'd have this family business that we could grow together, or sell or ..." His voice drifted off and he turned his head to gather himself. I put my arm around his waist and lowered my head to his chest.

"That was my motivation, to hand the keys to you. I never had anyone give me much, and I just wanted to give all of this to you so you wouldn't have to work like I did."

He paused again, his eyes transfixed on me, glassy like big dark marbles.

"But it's all bullshit, Parker," he said, a small smile appearing. "I want you to promise me that you won't waste your life in a boardroom. Go live your life. Explore every corner and do what makes you happy. Make some memories."

I shook my head. No.

"Daddy, you're going to be okay," I muttered, lifting my head up, my lip quivering. "You have to be okay. I don't want any of this, Daddy. I can't run the business like you. I just want you to be okay."

He lifted his hand, reaching out for me, and I took it in mine. A lone tear rolled down his cheekbone, which had become more prominent and chiseled from his weight loss.

"You remember that time we took Willy's little boat over to Mattituck?" he asked. Mattituck is a small beach town on Long Island's north shore.

"Sure," I said. "We found that beach. No people. We had it all to ourselves."

"When I was a kid, Parker, I'd go to the beach in Connecticut, and on clear days I could look across the Sound and see Long Island. I dreamt of having a boat. Of exploring all that water. Taking you there, together, just the two of us, and finding that beach with all those smooth rocks and the bunker jumping. I think about that day all the time. I didn't know it then but I had reached my goals. I'd accomplished my dream."

Daddy fought for another month, gaining enough strength to leave the hospital. We set him up at his small beach house on the shores of Long Island Sound, not far from the beach he fished as a young man. I had his bed placed by the window so he could stare at the body of water that called to him all those years ago.

He died in his sleep, just as the sun was coming up.

About three weeks after Daddy passed, my Uncle Willy, whom I'd known my entire life, gave me a key to a safety deposit box. When I got to the bank some time later and opened the box, I found Daddy's will and a typed, one-page letter addressed to me.

Dear Parker,

I wish we had had more time. But while my time is up, yours is only beginning. I want you to promise me you'll finish college. I never went to college and it always pissed me off that these college kids thought they were smarter than me. I know you have a love of books and culture. Don't let that questioning of things go to waste. Always search for the answers and enjoy the rest of your time in school.

I have made several business arrangements that you need to be aware of. I have worked out a deal to sell the company to the employees who have helped me build it. They know the business and they deserve the chance to move it forward. If you would like to be involved, there will always be a place for you, but I never saw you as the suit-and-tie type.

There is money set aside for some of our cousins, friends of mine and other people who are important to me, but the majority of the proceeds from the sale of the business will be placed in a trust for you. I don't want you to squander it, but I do want you to enjoy it. Make your dreams a reality, and watch out for piranhas who try to take advantage of you. Don't be stupid with this gift. Don't waste it on drugs or booze. I want you to be happy, Parker, so live the life you want to. Live a life with your feet in the sand or on the deck of a boat. Climb mountains. Make music. Do it all. And always remember that I love you.

- Daddy

I had inherited his dream of going out to sea. I vowed to continue his search. To hunt for fish in all of the world's oceans. To build a quiver full of memories and a web of friendships that crossed the globe.

CHAPTER THREE

El Chupacabra

Chupacabra (pronounced Chew-Pah-Kah-Bra): n. From the Latin chupar "to suck" and cabra "goat," quite literally the "goat sucker." A mythological creature purported to exist in Latin America. Said to have roots in Puerto Rico, this gargoyle-looking, nocturnal bloodsucker hops through the night, devouring livestock and terrorizing farmers. It's also a popular nickname for the penis.

A childhood friend of mine decided to build himself a giant, eight-bedroom home on the quiet north coast of the Dominican Republic. It didn't make sense to me at the time, but after my first visit, I could see why Monte chose to pick up and head down to the D.R.

Monte came from a wealthy family. He and I had run amuck throughout our adolescent years. We went to Catholic school together, and there was no dare we didn't attempt, no girl we didn't talk to and no rule we didn't break. How we survived, I do not know.

When Monte first bought this property, he was about the only gringo in the tiny town of Cabarete. But he pulled together the funds and purchased a swath of land right on the Atlantic Ocean. He built himself a sprawling villa with an infinity pool that seemed to reach out and lick the ocean waves. He planted gardens full of exotic flowers and fruits. Every room featured incredible views of the longest white-sand beach I'd ever seen.

A never-ending supply of delicious chicas fulfilled his lustful appetite, and some decent fishing for dorado, tuna and marlin curbed the need to travel in search of fish. Monte had found himself a quiet paradise, and he planted his flag.

Monte is no small guy. He played fullback while studying philosophy at Columbia. It wasn't during Columbia's notorious losing streak, but Monte's football career never really amounted to much. He enjoyed chasing women and filling his belly with beer more than waking up at five in the morning for two-a-day practices.

When he got down to the D.R. he towered over most every local. He's about 6-foot-2 and a solid 250 pounds. The local men feared him. He had a few tussles that made him a bit infamous around town. According to one story, Monte confronted a local guy who had robbed his villa. Everyone knew this guy had stolen some gardening equipment from Monte's place. The guy took the stuff and stashed it in his meager *casa* outside of town. Monte's staff told him about the missing equipment and the likely thief, so Monte went over there to reclaim his tools. The stuff was there, but the guy denied stealing it. He said he had found them, and decided to take them home. Thievery rule number one: If you get caught with stolen goods, say you found them. It works great.

This guy was in a Brugal-induced bluster. The local rum had built up his bravado. The thief picked up a shovel and swung it at Monte's torso. Monte grabbed the shovel with his left hand and damn near removed the idiot's head with his right. The contact of Monte's fist snapped the poor bastard's neck back like a catapult and knocked him out cold. Monte loaded up the gardening equipment in the back of his truck, tossed the thief in the passenger seat and dropped him off at the local doctor's office on his way home — Monte was no savage.

Word of this altercation quickly blew through town and men began to steer clear of the large gringo. The local women, on the other hand, favored Monte. They loved his blue eyes, his dark, straight hair and his generosity. Monte became the town's white Casanova, bedding women most every night. It didn't take long for him to gain a reputation around town, and the ladies started calling him "Gallo," which is Spanish for "rooster." The nickname referred to the moans and yips he would let out during his cock-a-doodle-do coitus crescendo. In the span of a year, the entire town began calling him Gallo, as did I and a bunch of our friends.

I'd head down to hang out with Gallo and raise some hell at least three or four times a year. This part of the Dominican

Republic is far removed from the all-inclusive resorts you find in Punta Cana and Puerto Plata. Those places are filled with fat tourists who just come to stuff their faces and point at the locals through the windows of their air-conditioned shuttle buses while they shake their heads at the poverty. They have no idea what they're missing. Cabarete is a utopia with undisturbed beaches, waterfalls and a local population of warm people content to live a quiet, laid-back existence. It's Caribbean gold, and Monte truly outdid himself here. He built a house worthy of mention in a home-décor magazine. The Spanish-style villa was built from local stone and painted white, with local hardwoods used as trim. The windows were two feet taller than any man I'd ever met. The ocean breezes cascaded through the simply appointed bedrooms. Private baths featured outdoor showers with lush foliage so you could hear the ocean as you bathed. You could enjoy the crystal blues of the ocean from any room in the house, and the tall ceilings seemed to make the ocean sounds echo throughout the foyer. Monte had built himself a Caribbean castle.

But living alone in an eight-bedroom villa can get boring. So, Gallo got himself a dog, a giant Rottweiler he named Elvis. The dog was massive with a head like a cast-iron Dutch oven. Elvis lived for Gallo. They were always together. They'd ride through town in Monte's Toyota Land Cruiser, with Elvis' big head out the window, his tongue spewing drool like Hansel and Gretel's trail of breadcrumbs. Unfortunately, Elvis didn't like many other people. The big, black beast became a good watchdog, but he liked to make a game out of harassing the gardeners. The workers would run like hell when Elvis came at them, tongue bouncing out of his snarled snout. They'd jump in the pool. Like that'd work. Elvis swam like a hippo. They'd haul themselves up trees and scream at the massive drooling beast. Elvis didn't bite many of them. He preferred to flop on top of them and pin them down like a wrestler.

Elvis was the only dog I knew that could climb a fucking palm tree. Seriously. It'd have to be one of those palms that grew a bit parallel to the ground, but the 120-pound slobbering pooch worked his way up there, hugging the tree with his front paws like a bartender going after a keg of beer. Getting down the tree was a different story. Elvis would lose his grip and slide down like a very ungraceful grizzly.

On one of my visits, I missed my connection in Miami and ended up spending the night in South Beach. I found a room at a trendy boutique hotel right on Ocean Drive and proceeded to get entangled in a bottle of rum. I progressed to some margaritas or mojitos, I don't quite remember, and made my way toward Ted's Hideaway, the only bar in South Beach worth drinking in unless you're one of those trendsetters who enjoy jumping velvet ropes and drink prices so high you have to finance your sweaty rum-and-Coke before you can actually suck one down.

I was sitting at the bar under the purple neon and making small talk with a fantastically dressed young Cuban waitress. (I swear, there are few things hotter than a good-looking Cuban woman. They look at you so sexily, and the movement in their ass when they walk away leaves you wishing they'd turn around.) I began chatting with the dapper guy in linen pants sitting next to me and it turned out he was a fellow angler.

Miami is ground zero for fishermen. You can't toss a quarter 10 feet without hitting somebody in the eye who likes to fish. About an hour later we decided to grab his skiff in Key Biscayne. We'd get some live shrimp and take a few drifts through Government Cut and try to catch a tarpon. I was 100 percent game — until I tried to stand up.

I'd no doubt forgotten to eat dinner, maybe even lunch, but my legs were in no shape to spend the next few hours bouncing around one of the country's busiest inlets. Plan B? Head back to the hotel, get something in my stomach and rethink the night's agenda. I told my new friend to give me a rain check and stumbled out into the night.

I didn't bother trying to hail a cab. The night air felt refreshing and I could hear the ocean. I began walking up Ocean Drive back toward my hotel. I was feeling good. Happy. Invincible. I made some small talk with a handful of cute tourists as I meandered north. Then I found a little pizza shop and grabbed a slice and a cold beer. There was an outside table so I plopped down to eat my pizza and watch the parade of gorgeous people walk by.

"Excuse me, do you know where the Delano is?" a young lady leaned over to ask me.

"Sure," I said, wiping some pizza sauce off my chin.

"Cool. Me and my friend are down from Chicago and we're staying at the Delano but I'm totally lost."

I looked around and saw no friend. My luck it'd be some dude wanting to toss me in a lake. But no, another cute young girl came back from the pizza counter, slice in hand, and sat next to the one asking me directions.

"I'll tell you what, my hotel is in the same direction. If you want, I can walk you girls down there," I said.

"Really?" she said and actually sounded excited about the offer. "Oh my God, that would be so awesome."

Of course I had no idea where the Delano was, but I figured we'd stumble across it at some point.

We finished our pizza, ordered up one more beer, then hit the road. The two girls, Monica and Melissa, which I only remember because I kept calling them M and M, had just graduated from college and were spending the last of their carefree days down in Miami before hitting the corporate think tanks in Chicago. They were cute. Not overly hot, but cute in a Midwestern way. Monica was brunette and thin while Melissa was dirty blond with huge tits. I had a hard time talking to Melissa, what with those rockets staring at me, but Monica and I hit it off. We chatted and walked.

I wanted another drink and convinced the girls to head into the bar of one of the hotels on Ocean Drive. I promised to buy the first round, and they were happy to oblige. We made our way through the bar, and just as we walked past the outside tables, I heard a cry that stopped me cold.

"What the fuck was that?" I asked.

"Got me," Monica said. "Sounded like someone just broke their ankle or something."

There it was again — a loud cry that sounded somewhat akin to a baby with a raging case of colic. The noise led me to a large cage parked in the hotel's back courtyard. There in the cage, sitting on a propped-up branch sat the strangest little creature I'd ever seen. It was about the size of a 10-week-old lab puppy. It had large, pointy ears like Yoda, a light furry coat, eyes that glowed orange in the dim-lit courtyard, miniature human-looking hands and a tiny little nose that could've been on a cat.

"What the hell are you?" I asked the little creature. Then it opened its cute little mouth and let out a cry that shook my soul.

In two swift hops, the animal was clinging to the cage right in front of my face. It tilted its little pointy head as it checked me out and extended its baby monkey paw out of the cage, offering up a handshake. I put out my finger and he softly grasped it, then scared the shit out of me with another startling cry. The little guy seemed to find my jumps hilarious, so he kept on screeching and I kept jumping.

I made my way back to the bar where the girls had ordered up a bottle of wine.

"What's that in the cage?" I asked the bartender.

"Ah, the bush baby," he said.

I gave him a confused look. "I've never heard of such a thing," I said.

"Yeah, I think they're from Africa or something. I know it's a primate, one of the smallest in the world, I think. The owner has a thing for unusual pets. I'm not sure how he got it."

"Where's the owner?" I asked.

The bartender pointed to a tall, thin man at a table with several well-dressed South Beach fellas, which Daddy would've called "poof-tahs." They had a flamboyant look about them.

I walked up to the table and extended my hand just like the bush baby. "I'm Parker McPhee," I said. "Tell me about your bush baby."

"What would you like to know, Mr. McPhee?" he asked as he looked me up and down in a way that made me a bit uncomfortable.

"Mostly I want to know how much."

"The animal is not for sale," he said.

"I'll give you ten grand. Cash."

A pause fell over the table in one of those record-scratching moments. The owner's flowery buddies looked at him, waiting for an answer.

"Let me get you the cage," he said, a smile appearing on his face.

I got so tied up in the purchase of my new pet that I completely forgot about Monica and Melissa. They were already talking to two other guys by the time we got the bush baby buttoned up in his little carrying case and I made it back to the bar. I asked them if we were squared up on the tab, and they seemed more than content to stay with their new friends, so I hurried on back to my hotel room to play with Bushie.

The next morning I awoke to two loud noises: an ear-popping, high-pitched screech and a bang at the door. What the fuck?

"Sir, please take care of that child!" someone yelled from the hallway. "Guests are threatening to call child services."

"We're fine, we're fine," I said.

Bushie was tense, looking frightened and unkempt. There was monkey piss all over the place. What the fuck was I going to do with this little guy? I figured it needed something to eat, so I picked up my computer to find out about the bush baby's diet. According to Wikipedia, they eat insects, leaves and fruit. That shouldn't be too hard in Miami, I figured.

After scoring some bananas, Fruit Roll-Ups and apples from the concierge, I sat down to come up with a plan. The entire reason behind my purchase was to give the bush baby to Monte as a gift. I figured the Dominican climate would be perfect for the monkey creature, and I could picture Monte walking through town with this big-eyed primate on his shoulder.

Getting an exotic animal out of the States and into a foreign country posed a bit of a challenge. I figured I would dope little Bushie with a sliver of a Valium, wrap him in a hotel towel and put him in the carrying case, which was one of those puppy bags you see ladies using to carry a Yorkie. I'd tell the airline folks it was a puppy and go for it. But they sort of frown upon you boarding a plane heading out of the country with an animal that looks like a cross between a monkey, a squirrel and a bat. Even if I made it through the airport, I didn't have any papers or even know what papers you'd need to bring a nonindigenous species into the country. But I did have a good bit of cash on me. I'd figure

something out or just bribe my way through customs. How hard
could it be?

I pushed about one-eighth of a Valium into a banana chunk
and fed it to Bushie. He wolfed it down and put his little hand out
for more. Twenty-five minutes later he folded down his Yoda ears
and curled up into an adorable little puff ball. I tucked him into his
cage. Snug as a bug.

We hailed a cab and headed to the airport. My flight to the
D.R. was at 1 p.m. so I had some time. I went up to the counter
and asked for a ticket to Chicago.

"I'll need a dog pass," I said, motioning to the little case. "Poor
guy isn't doing well and we're headed home to see the vet."

The middle-aged flight employee didn't say a word. I was
thinking I'd get a sympathy "aww" or something to that effect.
Nothing. Not a peep. Total tunnel vision. I probably could've died
right there and she wouldn't have even noticed.

"I got a flight at four," she said.

"I'll take it."

With my domestic boarding pass in hand, I made it through
security almost too easily. They never opened the case. I told them
I had a dog in there and they let me carry it through the metal
detector. An unenthusiastic agent buzzed me with a wand and that
was that.

Once past security I threw out the Chicago boarding pass and
headed toward my international flight. Bushie was still out cold.
With my priority boarding, I was in the first wave of passengers to
get on the plane. I found my seat, next to the window, and put
Bushie under the seat in front of me. No muss, no fuss. No one
even asked me about the pet carrier. The flight attendant offered
me a blanket, which I took and stuffed in front of the carrier so all
you could see was a blob of blue blanket and my canvas carry-on. I
decided to check my other bag even though it was small enough to
fit in the overhead. I always joke that I'm the type of guy who can
fit his baggage in the overhead ... literally and figuratively. It's total
bullshit, but sometimes it works with the ladies.

I pulled out a magazine and started to relax. A bearded guy
wearing a turban sat down next to me. We made the congenial

nods at each other but didn't say much. I hate people who want to befriend everyone sitting next to them on a public form of transport. Unless I'm drunk, odds are I won't speak to you. Nothing personal, I just don't find small talk entertaining. Even when the blabber escalates to middle talk it pretty much bores me, unless you're cute or have a nice rack. I'll suffer through two hours of biblical rhetoric to stare at perfect breasts.

The plane departed, and once we hit altitude and leveled out, I felt like I might actually pull this off. I took a deep breath and let myself slowly unwind.

The words on the pages of the magazine began to blend and I started to doze. Just as my eyes began to close I caught a moving blur in my peripheral vision. The man next to meet let out a muffled scream as if he had just felt a spider crawling on his neck. I blinked away the sleep and the vision that registered was too funny not to laugh at. Somehow, Bushie had managed to open the zipper on the cage with his miniature hand, leapt out and was clinging to the turban on the head of my neighbor. I was looking at a miniature, doped-out King Kong hanging onto a Q-tip.

"Oh my God," I said, reaching out to grab little Bushie. "I'm so sorry."

My neighbor was sort of frozen, head tilted a bit to the right.

"It's quite all right," he said in a British accent. "I've smuggled a few things in my day."

I smiled at him and offered to buy him a drink.

"Not much of a drinker really, but I think I'll make an exception," he said. "Dewar's, neat."

Luckily Bushie didn't let out a screech. He was still dopey from the Valium. I liked him in this state. He was quiet and all cuddly and clingy. His little hands wrapped around my fingers, and his eyes glassed over. I broke off another crumb from a Valium, wrapped it in a Fruit Roll-Up and gave it to the little guy. We still had a good hour left in the flight, and I didn't want Bushie to make any noise in Customs, which can take forever in Santo Domingo.

Lane, my neighbor, turned out to be an interesting guy. He was an architect working on a large golf project in Punta Cana. He liked to fly-fish and we talked about fishing for rainbow trout until

34

the plane hit the ground. Lane fishes Russia's Kamchatka Peninsula for trophy rainbows that suck down dry flies all day.

"It's like Alaska was 50 years ago," he said. "Wild, unfished and a fucking adventure just to get there."

I was sold.

He invited me on a trip. To get there you must fly in a decommissioned Russian military chopper loaded down with inflatable drift boats, camp stoves, tents, fly gear, food and enough vodka to swim in. You float several rivers over the course of a week, catching 24-inch rainbows till your arms fall off. We exchanged contact info. That's how it happens in the fishing world. Sometimes you meet your future best friend while sipping scotch on a plane after a monkey mounts your neighbor's turban.

We touched down in Santo Domingo, and the humidity hit me hard as I deplaned and walked down one of those drivable staircases and onto the tarmac. Bushie was still curled up in a ball. Quiet as a mouse. I made my way to Customs, armed with $100 bills. When in doubt, flash some cash.

I figured I'd just play stupid and pay my way through. It's worked before. I mean it wasn't like I was carrying a kilo of coke or something. It's just a monkey ... well, a bush baby.

I draped a long-sleeve shirt over the pet carrier so you couldn't really see what it was. It just looked like a small duffle bag.

I purchased my tourist card with no incident. Step one complete. Next, I picked up my checked bag from the carousel and walked up to the line for the Customs counter to get my passport stamped. I was waved in by a cute girl with terrible bright-blue eye shadow. I smiled widely. She hardly looked at me. She took my documents, stamped the passport and welcomed me to the Dominican Republic. That was it. I was in. Holy shit, I had just smuggled an African bush baby into the D.R. I walked out with a fat grin on my face and sure as shit, there was Monte. He waved me down and embraced me in a giant bear hug.

"Parker McPhee, you old son of a bitch!" he said. "I got three girls in the car, two at the house and a boat fueled up and ready to hit the water."

"Thank you, my friend. I got something for you too," I said.

"But it's a surprise."

It's a good two-hour run straight across the country to the steeper, lusher northern coast. The girls kept us good company as Monte's driver zipped us along a freshly paved highway. We drank Presidente beers as cold as dry ice and played with the ladies.

"So what's the surprise?" Monte asked. "You didn't go and get another walking dildo, did you? Remember when you pulled that on Sister Elizabeth? Oh man, I thought she'd die right there."

"Nope, no toys this time," I said. "This little surprise breathes on its own."

Monte looked at me with his head tilted like a puppy in deep wonderment. "You can't bring live animals into this country, Parker," he said.

"Like I could pull something like that off. Come on, Gallo, I'm not that stupid."

Finally, after a missed flight, an overnight in Miami, the two-hour flight to Santo Domingo and subsequent two-hour drive, the destination was slowly appearing. Monte's castle had never looked so beautiful. He'd added more gardens since my last visit, and as we pulled up, a gorgeous, caramel-skinned woman in a string bikini stood waiting for us with cocktails. I turned to Monte, smiling like a kid.

"Welcome home, old boy," he said.

I took my luggage to a room upstairs, and the official greeter wasn't far behind me. Just as I put my things in the closet I heard a light tap at the door. I opened it up and there she was, smiling seductively, holding another drink for me.

"Gracias," I said. She handed me the drink with one hand and placed her other hand behind my neck, pulling me to her soft lips for a long kiss. My dick rose to attention in record speed and tapped her on the thigh. She kept kissing me, opening her mouth and touching my lips with her tongue. She lightly took ahold of my cock and moved me into the room, heading for the bed. With a slight shove, I was on my back, her on top of me. She was still smiling.

"You like what you see?" she asked. I nodded emphatically. She reached behind her neck and untied the string holding up her bikini top. The fabric fell slowly, revealing two of the most beautiful breasts I'd ever seen. Teardrop shaped, coconut colored with Hershey Kisses for nipples. She leaned down, placing one breast right in my mouth. Delicious. She began to move and grind on me. Soft and sexy. Her hands meandered toward my cock when I heard a rustle in the closet.

Oh shit, I thought to myself. She lifted her head for a second, her thick midnight curls dangling in my face. They smelled like lavender.

"Don't stop," I said. "It's just my monkey."

"Moan-key?" she giggled.

I flipped her over and got on top of her. The rustle got louder and then the sound moved. Oh fuck, he's out of the cage. I tried to speed this up, predicting what was about to go down. I felt something land on the bed. No! Bushie was face to face with the girl. They made eye contact and that's when the silence was broken by two of the loudest screams ever recorded in Latin America. She screamed, Bushie screamed, I screamed. We all screamed.

"Shut up! For the love of God, shut up, you're going to scare him," I begged.

Useless words. The sight of little Bushie struck such fear in the beautiful girl that she became uncontrollable. She bounded out of bed, beautiful breasts bouncing like perfectly weighted water balloons. I couldn't take my eyes off them. Swaying so perfectly. I wished I could achieve such a flawless presentation when fishing a streamer on moving water.

She tripped over my bag and crab-walked out of the room on all fours, still screaming.

Bushie continued to cry nervously but dropped the volume considerably. He made it to the top of the curtain rod and was watching me move about the room, my hard-on sticking out of my pants like a tree limb (well, maybe a decent twig). I pulled a mango out of the fruit basket on the ottoman and used it to lure Bushie off the curtains. He crawled down and made it to the bed.

"Poor Bushie," I said. "You've had quite a day."

I could hear the commotion downstairs. Fast Spanish being tossed around like tomatoes in a food fight. I managed to coerce

Bushie into my hands. He grabbed onto me from the side of my torso and I slid one arm around him. His little heart was nearly beating out of his chest.

I slowly walked down the stairs, whispering to Bushie, trying to calm him. As I rounded the corner near the kitchen, I could see Monte, the beautiful girl, another girl and Antonio, Monte's villa manager. Antonio saw me first and pointed at the small animal clinging to me.

Monte turned around and I watched him work to focus on exactly what this animal clinging to me was. Monte moved in closer, got near Bushie, and examined his small Yoda ears, soft coat, yellowish eyes and miniature hands.

"That's the coolest thing I've ever fucking seen," Monte said.

I gave Monte a big smile and said "Surprise!"

The staff didn't like the looks of Bushie. They'd never seen an animal like this and they feared it. I heard two uses of the word *chupacabra*. They thought little Bushie might be a bloodsucking monster.

Monte thought my surprise was adorable and I think the feeling was mutual. Bushie took to Monte instantly, climbing up Monte's wide back and perching himself on his right collarbone. We made our way to the veranda to look at the ocean and catch up. Things settled down and Antonio brought us a small ice chest with some Presidente beers chilling inside. It felt great to be back in the D.R.

We cracked a couple of the beers and fed Bushie some fresh fruit. After about my third beer, the sun began to fade off and I made the very stupid mistake of asking about Elvis, Monte's troublesome Rottweiler.

"Fucking Elvis," Monte said. "That damn dog has caused me more grief than you'd ever know. He's gotten into killing cattle. I've had to buy three dead cows in the last two weeks. Can you believe that?"

"Wow," I said. "He can take down a cow?"

"Oh yeah, and these so-called ranchers know I have money so it's almost like they feed the sick cows to Elvis so they can come to me and collect. I wonder where old Elvis is right now. Elvis! Come here, boy!"

I looked at Bushie, who had climbed off Monte and was digging into some fruit in a bowl at the edge of the table. His little fingers were all sticky with mango juice.

"Hear that?" Monte asked. It sounded like a thoroughbred rounding the corner about to run head-on into us. As the sound grew louder and louder I feared for Bushie.

"Monte, no!" I yelled, but it was too late. Elvis came flying around a corner of the house at full speed. He lost his footing on the slate patio and slid into the chair leg, taking me down. The dog's momentum pushed him into the table and he sideswiped a table leg, causing the entire wrought-iron table to topple over. As the long rectangular table flipped, it catapulted little Bushie into the air like a furry, screeching cannonball. He flew like Superman over Monte's fence and into the dense foliage outside the property.

I clamored to my feet, my shirt soaked in the beer I was drinking, and ran toward the main entrance of the house to search for Bushie. The sun had just about disappeared by now and so had my little bush baby.

That night a group of twenty-somethings were dancing to some reggaeton at Humps, an open-air watering hole on the beach not far from Monte's house, when a pointy-eared, grey-skinned animal flew in from the rafters and landed on the bar. According to eyewitnesses, the strange animal had fear in its eyes, and blood on its mind. It held its tiny human hands to its sides and let out a chorus of screams that could be heard for miles. The dancing crowd fled the bar in a stampede. One man was not so lucky. He slipped on spilt rum, knocking himself out cold. The chupacabra pounced on him, clinging to his side and sucking the blood from his neck. The ill-fated man was found days later in a stupor on the beach. His hair had gone white and he'd developed a nervous twitch. For years, this tiny chupacabra tormented the good people of the Dominican Republic's north coast. Rumor has it the bloodsucker came from Miami.

CHAPTER FOUR

No Banana

I f every airport had the same level of security as Cartagena, Colombia, flying the not-so-friendly skies would be a much safer experience.

I walked off the Avianca Airlines flight onto the jetway, and just as I was about to step into the fluorescent-lit, air-conditioned comfort of the small international airport, a teenaged soldier dressed in fatigues pointed the barrel of a machine gun at me. It stopped me dead and I immediately wished I hadn't enjoyed those four Havana Club-and-Cokes, but it was *Havana Club*. I'd never tasted the Cuban rum. I figured if Hemingway drank it, I might as well try it. I liked it a bit too much, I suppose. Dark and rich. Cuba Libre!

The puerile soldier used the gun like a finger and motioned me over to a small folding table. I moved out of line while the boy in green, who was all of 16, let several passengers freely pass into the airport. (I could tell his age by his wispy moustache that looked more like spread-out hackle on a poorly tied dry fly than facial hair.)

My feet had yet to touch actual Colombian soil, and there I was being patted down as gloved soldiers rooted through my bags. All of those fears about traveling to Colombia that I had brushed off slowly flooded back into my thoughts. Was this a shakedown? Did someone plant something in my bag? Why the fuck didn't I buy travel insurance?

The man flipped the bag over on the table, dumping out the contents of my carry-on. My usual mishmash of prescribed drugs rattled onto the plastic table: Ambien and Valium for sleep, Xanax for its varied jollies, multivitamins, Excedrin migraine, muscle relaxers and one little blue pill just in case the Havana Club rendered Little Parker lifeless. He pulled out my inshore fly box, two fly reels (a nine-weight Abel and a 12-weight Tibor

Gulfstream), a pair of titanium pliers, fishing gloves, sunblock, a *Penthouse*, a half-full bottle of water, an iPhone, spools of tippet and fly line, a bandana that stank like dried bonefish slime, my passport and travel documents, a paperback journal, wallet, clean shorts and a roll of toilet paper. The smell of the bandana must've got him. As quickly as he poured out the contents, he squashed them all back into the canvas bag.

I took a deep breath, popped one of the Valiums, finished off the water bottle and moved toward immigration. It took me nearly two hours to get through the various checkpoints and obtain all of the necessary stamps and papers to enter the country. I was annoyed but impressed. How could Colombia be such a dangerous place if they put everyone through such a rigmarole just to get in? Or did they only treat gringo idiots like myself this way? I guess it didn't really matter. I was in.

I proceeded with some caution toward the exit door. The usual aggressive cab drivers tried to help me with my luggage. I waved them off like a halfback punching out a stiff arm. I didn't have much baggage. I brought one roller bag and one carry-on. My usual gear. I had packed only one nice shirt and a decent pair of pants; the rest of my belongings were for fishing.

Going out in Cartagena meant wearing a tight pair of black dress pants, a pressed cotton button-down and some fancy shoes. This town, or city rather, is a tourist mecca for rich Europeans, South Americans and everyone else who isn't afraid to enter the country.

Cocaine czar Pablo Escobar was gunned down in 1993. Unfortunately for the good people of Colombia who are trying to resurrect a tourism industry, the sociopathic drug lord lives on in countless movies and documentaries. That notoriety has helped keep Americans from visiting this delightful colonial city for decades, and for that much, I should thank Pablo. Few places have more inherent charm than the old city of Cartagena. It's also a great spot to hide from loud, obnoxious heathens from Omaha.

A young man dressed like a dock rat from Fort Lauderdale holding a piece of cardboard with "Parker McPhee" written in black magic marker stood just behind the mass of cabbies, tour guides and swindlers. As I got closer I could see little rings patterned across the brown cardboard. This kid had made the sign from the bottom of a case of beer.

"I'm Parker," I said, extending my hand.

The young man took off his polarized sunglasses and I could tell he spent a lot of time on the water. Reverse raccoon eyes. The rest of his face was a chocolaty tannin brown, but the skin behind those frames was as white as the underside of a doe's tail.

"Nice to meet you. I'm Junior," he said, in perfect English. Not a lick of an accent.

I nodded. "You sound like you're from the States," I said.

"I just graduated from the University of Alabama," Junior responded.

"Ah, right on," I said. "Some cute girls in Birmingham ... Roll Tide!"

"Tuscaloosa," Junior said.

"Oh yeah, that's what I meant."

He gave me a small grin, scooped up my luggage and we made our way to his Toyota SUV. Junior's father, Carlos Gaviria, and Daddy were old friends and business partners. Carlos came from a wealthy Colombian family and like all of his brothers and sisters, he went to school in the States. But unlike his siblings, Carlos wanted only one thing, to become a mariner and build boats. He studied at the SUNY Maritime College in the Bronx and fished whenever he could.

Our fathers met when Carlos was in the States attending college in New York. On one of his fishing excursions, Carlos drove down to the Connecticut shoreline hoping to catch some striped bass and the hard-to-find, sea-run brown trout. Carlos bumped into Daddy as the two men walked down Riverside Avenue with fishing rods, in the wealthy town of Westport. Daddy was wearing hip boots and carrying a five-gallon bucket in one hand and two fishing rods in the other. They had both read an article in one of the local newspapers about targeting the sea-run browns from a tiny piece of public waterfront property. These migratory fish make their way into tidal creeks and streams from Long Island Sound to spawn. Once they hatch the fry must slip past voracious striped bass, bluefish, fluke and other predators for a chance at survival in the saltier waters. They are known to be finicky eaters and drive anglers crazy. Carlos actually caught one, as the story goes, and Daddy shadowed him the rest of the day. They were both in their twenties.

Carlos got his degree in naval architecture and ended up back in Cartagena, where he purchased a marina and turned it into the largest boatyard in the country. He built his own vessels, designed the hulls, wrote the CAD drawings, constructed his own molds, laid the fiberglass, ran the wires, installed the power. He could've paid others to do all of this work, but he loved it too much.

The boatyard made Carlos a rich man on his own accord. The money was in engine repairs, bottom paint and refits, but Carlos loved building boats. He constructed mostly center consoles, and a few inboard sport-fishers. Much like an artist, Carlos found it difficult to part with his true masterpieces, but he sold them here and there. Carlos looked at boats differently than you or me. When he inspected a vessel, he placed his head against the hull to look down the side of the boat and get a sense of her lines, imagining how she might perform in a head-sea. He placed his hands on the fiberglass to feel for bumps and flaws. He admired the curves and flare of the bow. Functional art. That's what Carlos called a perfect boat.

Every year for more than two decades, Daddy went down to Colombia in October to fish with Carlos in the Cartagena de Indias International Marlin Tournament. Now that Daddy was gone, Carlos invited me to take his place.

Junior and I left the airport in his SUV and headed toward the Old City. This portion of Cartagena dates back to the 14th century. Cartagena came to prominence during the peak of the gold trade in the Colonial era. The Spanish armadas coveted the place for its location. As gold came out of Peru, it went through Cartagena before making its way to Europe. Massive runs of ships with their bellies full of gold attracted pirates like remoras to sharks.

The Spaniards built forts all over the city. They protected the entrance of the harbor with hidden obstacles below the surface of the water. You'd run aground if you didn't know where you were going. And if that didn't get you, one of the many canyon turrets would do you in as you pushed closer to shore. No other Caribbean city is so fortified.

Cartagena's Castillo San Felipe de Barajas is a masterpiece of military engineering. The fort sits on a hill, a good spot to pick off pirates. But when the pirates got smart, they attacked from behind, from land, and caught the Spaniards with their pants down. Pirates loved to loot this city and tear down all of the crosses and signs of Catholicism after they got tired raping and pillaging.

Junior offered to take me to the fort to check it out, but I was more thirsty than curious.

"I want to meet some girls and get a drink," I said.

"We're fishing at 5 a.m. tomorrow."

"So? A few drinks will be fine. C'mon, man. You're a young guy. Roll Tide, right?"

He gave me a confused look and shook his head. "Dude, you're going to get me in trouble."

Junior's instructions were to take me to the hotel where I would get a tour of the place, eat dinner and retire to my suite. The hotel was deep within the walled city, a converted nunnery from the 1500s. It looked pretty spectacular from the window of Junior's SUV as we sped past. I had sweet-talked my young chauffeur into heading to Boca Grande at the mouth of the bay, where young tourists party into the wee hours. I figured we'd grab some drinks and take it from there.

We found at a quaint taqueria with open-air seating. I walked across the street to a little liquor store and bought a liter of Havana Club. We mixed it with Coke and went through about half of the bottle over dinner. I ordered some tamales, rice, beans, chorizo and fried plantains.

Music pours out of every door in Cartagena. We poked our heads into various clubs to inspect the talent. We finally decided on an establishment of less than ideal repute and parked ourselves at a table. I had no idea where we were. All I knew was that my luggage was in the car, which was parked somewhere a few blocks away. Probably not the best spot to store my bags, but I wasn't worrying about it. I felt a healthy buzz looming over the situation like a light layer of mist hanging a few feet above the surf. The Valium from the airport had long washed away, and the rum-and-Cokes were making me frisky.

Junior and I waved down a waitress and I felt myself getting checked out. Gringos are easy targets for these girls. A few young ladies came over and whispered to Junior. He laughed, shook his head and began chatting with them in Spanish, leaving me asking, "What'd she say? What'd she say?"

"They want to know if you're American," he said. "They think you're Robert Downey Jr."

"Really? Shit, go with that, man. Wait. No, tell them I invented Google! They know Google, right? Everyone knows Google. Tell them I just bought a big house on the water and I'm looking for a girlfriend."

"Dude, you're crazy," Junior said.

"C'mon, just try it. If that doesn't work, we'll get them drunk."

Junior spoke, they all laughed and one of the girls moved over to the chair next to me. She was cute. Light skin and slick, black hair. Her eyes were so dark I couldn't determine where her pupil stopped and the iris started. She wore a lot of makeup. Even in the low light of the beach bar I could see layers of foundation powder, some of it cracked like Mona Lisa's chin. My excitement level began to wane. Her clothes were a bit too revealing. Lots of pink mesh and dark outlines. You could see the wires of her bra or corset or whatever it was like they were meant to be an accessory. And I don't like saying it, but there was a strange aroma coming from her. Bad perfume battling it out with body odor. An ugly fight that I wanted no part in.

One of my steadfast rules is to never go with the first girl who approaches you in a bar in a strange country where women approach guys looking for more than just a free drink. Sometimes this rule gets shoved under the rug. That's never a good thing.

I kicked Junior under the table.

46

"Get rid of her," I whispered.

She sensed my fleeting interest, shrugged her shoulders and opened her mouth to make some sort of surprised look, but all I saw was her teeth, two rows of yellowed corn kernels, a few of which were either eaten away or had fallen off the cob.

"That's it," I said and stood up. "I'm going to take a piss. Please get rid of these two by the time I'm back." I smiled at the girl and walked into the dim scene surrounding the bar.

I tried to keep a low profile, not wanting to gain the attention of any Colombian drug lords who might be hanging out even though it was pretty obvious this bar was filled with vacationing city folks. It had the typical beach-bar vibe with calypso-infused music, low lights and neon posters on the walls. But still, I made no eye contact — just worked my way toward the baño. I was moving along okay until my foot clipped the edge of a barstool and I lost my balance, falling onto my knees.

"Holy, fucking shit," I said as I nearly stumbled into what very well may have been the most beautiful girl I'd ever seen.

"Pardón?" she said, wincing her eyes with a twinge of disapproval.

Holy, fucking shit, I thought to myself, that's all you could come up with? I was frozen by her gaze. I stared into her eyes, admired her perfectly arched eyebrows and thick Liz Taylor eyelashes (young, hot Liz Taylor ... not the old, worn-out Liz.) I tried not to stare at her dark, black-coffee eyes. She was an Egyptian goddess dropped here, right onto a barstool in front of me. I shifted to one knee and took her hand.

"I'm Parker," I said. "Uh, mi nombre es ..."

"Hello, I'm Claudia," she said with a little laugh. "Are you asking me to marry you?"

"Holy shit, you speak English."

"Si, only a little." Her accent washed over me like a mountain stream. I suddenly felt the desire to write a song or a poem about her soft fingers and her silky flowing hair. But I'd never written a song or a poem.

Oh shit, I'm in trouble.

I bought Claudia a drink. She was waiting for a friend of hers, who, lucky for Junior, was a solid seven, about four notches up from the aromatic wire bra I was just talking to.

My eyes, however, were locked on Claudia. I inspected every inch of her, trying not to creep her out with my wanting stare, but I don't think it was working. She didn't have a single blemish on her. My gaze began at her toes. Nails manicured in a pastel yellow and exposed in a pair of worn, comfortable-looking sandals. Her legs were toned and smooth but not overly muscular. I accidentally brushed my leg against them a few times. Her skin was a healthy, slightly tanned brown. The color of light chocolate milk. She wore a short skirt, and it took all of my willpower to keep my hand from running up her leg and under that fabric. Her black tank-top didn't quite reach the skirt, leaving her flat tummy exposed, a perfectly shaped navel winking at me seductively.

Looking at her was near tortuous. I just wanted to touch her, smell her, taste her.

I drank two or three more cocktails, and Claudia kept inching closer, or maybe I was subconsciously creeping toward her. I wasn't sure which, but we were closing the gap between us, which was all that mattered. She's either torturing me, or she might actually like me, I thought. When she stood up to head to the bathroom, I stood up as well. The minutes she was gone sucked, and I feared she might not come back. But when she did I pulled her stool out for her, watched her smile at me and slid her back to the table. Her tongue peeked out and touched her top lip. More drinks.

At about 1:30 a.m. Junior started getting nervous.

"Parker, please, let's call it a night. My dad is going to go ape shit. He takes this tournament super serious. He'll be at the boat in a few hours, man. We have to call it a night."

"Go ahead, Junior," I said. "I'll see you in the morning."

"Are you nuts? I can't leave you here."

"Then hang out, man."

He grumbled and I figured we all needed a change of scenery.

"Ask them if they want to go to the beach," I said.

"I don't know man, this isn't Palm Beach," Junior replied.

"Just do it."

He spoke to the two girls in Spanish, his hands waving around a little bit like he was asking them if they wanted to go swimming. Claudia responded in a short sentence that shut up Junior and put his hands to rest. He sat up straight and turned to me, looking puzzled like he'd just gotten a whiff of sour milk.

"She wants to take you back to her place," he said.

"Shut up!"

"I don't know, man, we have to be a little careful here. Kidnappings still happen all the time. Muggings. Shake downs ..."

Claudia rattled something off in Spanish, and Junior responded. "She said she has the keys to a condo in one of the high-rises down the beach. My cousin works for a woman who lives there. It's a nice place."

"Go get your fucking car, Junior."

My legs were feeling a tad wobbly as we pulled up and parked beneath one of Cartagena's gleaming glass high-rises that dot the beach.

We popped out of Junior's SUV, and the air in the parking garage smelled a bit gassy. Noxious exhaust fumes swirling around the concrete burrow. It didn't agree with me. Claudia must've sensed some unease in my gait. She got close to my face and scanned my eyes, looking concerned. I wanted her closer. I smiled at her, and she smiled back. Her delicate pink lips parted to reveal two rows of white, gorgeous teeth as straight as train tracks.

"I'm okay," I said. She turned but paused for me to walk with her. I slightly bumped into her silkiness, and she snatched my right hand and placed it around her waist, intertwining my fingers in hers. As we waited for the elevator, she placed her other hand around my waist and faced me. Her black hair smelled like night-blooming jasmine planted by Eve herself. Temptress. I could feel the light tickles of her soft, waist-length, jet-black hair against my hands as they clung to her.

This was actually happening.

Junior was making small talk with Claudia's friend in the

elevator and it sounded a million miles away. My world had closed in on this brunette beauty. Claudia rubbed my hands with hers. I couldn't hold back any longer. I leaned into her, nuzzling my nose into her neck, making light kisses. She turned her head to the side to give me more access to her skin. I took the bait.

The elevator doors had opened, but I couldn't stop necking with Claudia. She tasted like salty gold.

"Break it up, Parker," said Junior. "The elevator door is open."

I reached down under Claudia's bottom and scooped her up in my arms. She let out a little scream of surprise and kicked her feet as she rattled off something in Spanish. She lost one of her sandals, which her friend retrieved as the elevator doors were about to close.

"Where'm I going?" I asked her, but not really caring. I would've taken her right there in the hallway.

She pointed to a door. I placed her on her feet and she inserted the key. I have no idea what the condo looked like. Claudia didn't turn on the lights; she just took me by the hand and led me to a bedroom. For a second, a wave of fear flooded over me. That, or a rush of rum, went to my head and retreated along with all the blood in my brain that got jostled around from scooping her up too quickly. This was all too easy. Maybe Claudia was playing me. Should I care? Can I still fuck her? Maybe if I can just fuck her it will be okay. Are there going to be goons waiting for me when the lights turn on? Will I wake up, wondering if she only existed in my dreams?

"Wait," I said to her. "I need to use the bathroom."

"Okay, Novio," she said, giggling. "It's here." She took a few steps down a hall and reached for a light switch. I felt my heart thump inside my ribcage, and I was a little out of breath as I stared at her hand that was about to make contact with the light switch. Things slowed down. My future hung on that switch like a guillotine, not to mention my cock. Once that light came on, there was a good chance everything would be ruined. The light may unearth a scene full of hate, violence and betrayal. I pictured two armed men sitting in the shadows, getting ready to bust out and charge me with the first sign of illumination. I could feel the sting of a gun's butt crashing against my skull. Blood dripping off my forehead. Claudia laughing, having lured another unsuspecting tourist into her trap.

I shut my eyes.

Click.

She flipped the switch. One eye opened. Brightness. No guns. No men. Just the most beautiful Colombian enchantress this side of the Amazon River. I threw my arms around her, lifting her off the floor and swung her in a circle. I placed her back down and gave her a long kiss, parting her lips with mine.

"Just give me a sec," I said, floating into the bathroom.

With the light on and no men waiting to kill me, I could breathe clear. I was going to be with this woman. I was going to pack her up in my suitcase and take her home with me to live forever. We'd make little babies with beautiful night-black hair and olive skin. They'd have long eyelashes, and we'd give them each a Latin name and an Anglo name. Robert Juan McPhee or Sarah Margarita. No, that sounds idiotic. Kaitlyn Rosita. That's better. We'd live somewhere warm. Florida or Mexico. Bogota or Barbados. I didn't care, just as long as I got to look at those espresso eyes every morning. She's mine now. She wants me.

I unleashed the tool, relieved the liquids, knocked off the dribbles and flushed. Then I made my way over to the sink and examined my face. My eyes — bloodshot, but not blood soaked. Feeling kind of wobbly now, I rinsed my face, dried off on a scratchy white washcloth next to the sink and ran my hand through my brown, billowy hair. The good thing about having wavy hair like I do is that it always looks kind of messy so there's never the worry of it looking messy. That's just the way it looks. I tried to straighten the nest atop my ears as best I could and pat down the cowlick in the back. It'd have to do. I checked my teeth. All clear. Staring at the mirror I realized it was actually a medicine cabinet and opened the door, just out of habit. All empty except one strange object: a syringe filled with a translucent liquid.

I pulled the needle out of the cabinet and held it against the light. *What the fuck?* The negative thoughts came pouring back. Claudia is going to drug me and harvest my body parts. Or maybe she's just diabetic? But she's so thin. She's so fucking gorgeous. Do gorgeous people get diabetes? What if she's a junkie? Nah, junkies would never leave their juice in such an obvious location. Wait, maybe I'm just imagining all of this. Maybe the rum is pushing the panic button in my brain. Pills. Did I take pills? I jammed my hands into my pockets and pulled out whatever was in there. Bills of mixed denomination, a lighter, a condom, three pills — one blue, one white and one hexagon-shaped. I shoved the hexagon pill into my mouth and swallowed. *Why the fuck did I just do that?* Fuck! Parker, control yourself goddammit! I breathed in deeply and let out a big, ugly cough.

Close the damn medicine cabinet, I told myself. *Take five.*

I shut the door, lied my head down on my forearm and hunched over the sink. I could feel my heart beating in my neck, the pulsating beginning to build in my temples as the RPMs increased. Adrenaline rushing now. Is the needle still in there? Maybe it's gone; maybe this is all a fucking dream, a hallucination. Can rum make you hallucinate? Thoughts raging, rum revolting, swirling like a hurricane in my gut. Don't retreat just yet, boys!

I opened the mirrored door and there it was. Small and lonely on a clear glass shelf. Just a few inches long and filled with something unknown. That's what was killing me. What is that in there? If she wanted to drug me, why would she have the syringe in here? It made no sense; this place makes no sense. I thought she wanted me. I still want her. Her jasmine-scented bosom. So soft and glorious. Her midriff waving me in, flat like a tarmac. I had to come up with a plan. I wanted to ignore the syringe. The fucking needle was cock-blocking me like a 400-pound bouncer. Claudia likes me, I thought. She wants me. She said so. Her hands were on me. Moving their way to my heart. No, maybe she wants my money. Fine, all women want money. I can give her fucking money. I have no problem with that. Just so long as she takes me too.

"Don't be so stupid," I said aloud to no one in particular, failing to make eye contact with the man in the mirror. "What about Junior? I can't let anything happen to him. He'll try to protect me. He may get hurt, or shot. Do it for Junior!"

One breath ... heart rate building. Second breath ... head bobbing to gain momentum. Third breath ... screaming something now!

I flung the door open and flew out of the baño like a jet stream, hoisting the syringe above my head, waving it like a soldier who'd lost control of his gun. Claudia screamed and leapt onto the bed to dodge my fumbling frame as I lurched into the dark.

"Why are you trying to kill me?" I yelled, and she screamed. Junior came flying into the room.

"What the hell, Parker?" he said.

"She's killing my pussy!" I said. *Wait, what*? The line of communication between thoughts and mouth was quickly breaking down. "I can't ... pussy! I don't want her to kill the pussy!"

My head collided with something hard, and I fell onto the mattress. Claudia jumped to the farthest corner of the bed and circled her hands around her knees, making herself into a protective ball. I leaned in toward her.

"Why, baby?" I asked. "Why do you want to kill me? I love you."

She punched me in the face.

I closed my eyes. Adrenaline crashing. Way down. Body s l u m p i n g.

Rum wins again.

Head throbbing with white light scorching my brain like mini lasers shot from some futuristic cataract-destroying weaponry. My entire body feeling heavy and lifeless. I aim to lift my head but nothing happens. No man, no Mr. Universe, could lift this 10-ton demon sitting atop my weakened neck.

My mouth, dry and caked, full of cola-soaked teeth that feel fuzzy against my tongue like they were wearing sweaters, began to open. I meant to speak, but not much came out. A grunt, I suppose, if you want to call it something.

I could hear some voices, far off, a foreign language. Music maybe. Like a dream, the voices were all around me, but the sounds bounced around the room too quickly for me to understand them in my current state. My eyelids felt like old hubcaps from a '59 Cadillac. Heavy and bright. The voices became a bit louder. Laughter.

The floor swayed to one side, and then the other. Senses started to zoom back into focus. Shirt soaked through. Head still throbbing. Throat in dire need of liquid. Cock limp. Heart hurts.

My eyes cracked open and I think my ears popped. Everything came into focus, the volume got turned way up and it was bright as all hell. Sun coming in through clear curtains, bouncing off white fiberglass and shiny aluminum and cutting through my retinas, making a beeline straight for the darkest depths of my brain pain. I attempted sitting up, but the right side of my face was stuck to a vinyl cushion. I slowly peeled my flesh from the sticky fabric. It sounded like gaffer's tape being pulled from a hairy carpet.

"Rough night, Parker?" someone asked.

I blinked several thousand times and squinted painfully to make out the shape of the man sitting at the helm chair. It was Junior's father, Daddy's old buddy, Carlos. I was on his boat. We were somewhere on an ocean. The sun was out. I wasn't dead.

"Good morning, Carlos," I said in a soft voice. "We catch anything?"

The tanned, bare-chested man shook his head and most likely rolled his eyes behind the polarized sunglasses he was wearing. He was sitting in a tall captain's chair behind the steering wheel at the helm of his classic, beautifully appointed 54-foot Bertram sportfisher. His head bobbed a bit as the big girl plowed through a slight chop. His frame was protected from the sun by the large hard top above him. He was in good shape for his age, early fifties. His hair was graying on the sides but otherwise thick, almost as thick as the mat of growth on his chest. A few gold chains hung around his neck. Not thick gangster chains, but they were flashy enough to show his passions. One held a 14-karat-gold sailfish with a ruby-red eyeball. The other, a coin of some sort. Shipwreck gold, I'm assuming. On either side of the steering wheel sat large monitors to run the onboard electronics. Many people of Carlos' wealth would hire someone to captain such a vessel, but not this man. He preferred to drive. He enjoyed the feel of the water beneath the boat. He relished the ability to set his own course. To succeed or fail on his own accord. He was truly a captain — out on the seas, searching for quarry.

Daddy used to tell me how Carlos could drive anything. Forklifts at the boatyard, small planes, tractors, motorcycles ... anything with an engine, Carlos could drive it. He was Neal Cassady and James Cook reincarnated. I was in good hands.

The hum of the diesels was hardly noticeable up here on the flybridge, making it much easier to talk.

"No," Carlos said, "we haven't caught anything yet, but you sure did." He leaned toward me and rubbed my cheek with his thumb. "Nice shiner."

There was a slight pause in the conversation as I worked to recall the evening's details. "I think we won," I said. He smiled.

"Listen, there are some very important people on the boat today. Successful businessmen who use my marina and pay me a lot of money to take care of their boats and keep their interests private, if you know what I mean. I need you to act appropriately."

"What's appropriate?" I asked. "We're in Colombia. There's got to be some leeway, I would think."

"Parker, I'm not joking," he said. "Tone down the language and just be polite. You can drink, you can smoke, you can piss off the transom, you can talk about women. That kind of stuff, I don't care. Just don't insult these men. Their egos outweigh their wallets, and their wallets are pretty fucking fat. You got me?"

"Si," I said. "Got anything to drink?"

"Down below."

I descended the ladder to the cockpit, taking my time and focusing through the bright sunlight so I wouldn't miss a rung. The big Bertram didn't move much in the light chop. I appreciated her stability. I even thanked her, I think. My feet settled on the fiberglass deck. All of that white fiberglass and the tinted glass of the salon door bounced light directly into my aching head. Sharp rays shot into my eye sockets like razorblades. I squinted my eyelids as tightly as possible, keeping them open just wide enough to provide enough vision to move toward the air-conditioned cabin. I put my hand out toward the fighting chair, mounted in the middle of the deck, and my fingers bumped into human flesh. It was Junior, dozing off with his hat over his eyes.

"Go fuck yourself, Parker," he said, not even moving an inch.

"I'm sorry, man. What the hell happened last night?"

He lifted his hat up, and his eyes were dark and wild with rage. He pounced at me, stopping just inches from my face, which was a good thing. My reflexes were in remission. He would've overcome me with no real effort whatsoever.

"Ahh," I yelled, crouching to ease the blow of the coming knuckles. "I already got punched in the face today, man. I'm sorry, alright. I'm sorry. Just tell me what happened!"

"You were an idiot — that's what happened. Everything was cool, you disappeared with Claudia, I was talking to her friend and next thing I know I hear all this banging and screaming. I thought you were getting jumped, man! I fly in there and you're fucking attacking *her*, man. You had some makeup pen or something in your hand and you weren't making any sense. I'm glad she hit you because I was about to."

"A makeup pen?" I asked. "No, she was going to stick me with a syringe, Junior. She wasn't the girl I thought she was."

"No, dude. That's where you're really wrong. She was that girl, and she was one of the hottest things I've seen in a long time. You fucked up, Parker. You fucked up bad. Now get the hell away from me, I'm not talking to you."

Dread, regret and embarrassment flooded my thoughts. I needed to get out of the sun and hide from myself for a bit.

I slid open the door to the salon of the boat, and the cool air gave me a much-needed hug. I stepped inside and was momentarily blinded by the change in brightness. I could make out a sofa to my left, and my body instinctively fell in that direction. I landed on my ass and my head sunk into the pillow. Over the thump of my pulsating headache, I made out some conversation. As the scene came into focus, I saw three men sitting at the dinette, playing cards and drinking sangria. One of them was smoking an awful-smelling, one-inch-thick cigar that looked like a big brown dildo in between his fingers.

"You must be Parker," said the youngest of the three men. He was handsome, movie-star handsome. His black hair was brushed back so it did not interfere with his pretty face. He was in his forties, with blue eyes, a muscular build and perfect skin. He was not wearing a shirt. He had on white top-siders and light-pink shorts that may have been red at one time. On his wrist I spotted a very expensive watch, stainless and Swiss. He looked like a Ralph Lauren model. I hated him immediately.

"Yes, sir," I said. "I'm Parker. Nice to meet you."

He smiled.

"We heard you had an interesting evening. The women in this town are something. Gorgeous, no? We've all been there," he said. "My name is Enrico and these are my friends Rafael and Javier."

Enrico pointed to the other two gentlemen as he introduced them. Rafael appeared to be in his late sixties. He wore dark glasses, a linen shirt and a wide-brimmed hat. Javier was younger, 50-something maybe, and the most genial-looking of the bunch. He wore a big smile below his bushy moustache. Even his eyes looked happy. I kind of hated him too.

Enrico said something to the other men in Spanish, and they all laughed and took turns looking back at me as they chattered, noting my overall dishevelment and undoubtedly speculating as to how my cheek became bruised. I closed my eyes, trying to ignore their noise.

"Parker, I hear you're a good fisherman," Enrico said. "We have not had a bite. What do you think we're doing wrong?"

I rubbed my eyes, looked up and noticed the most horrifying thing I've ever seen on a boat. On a shelf above Enrico's head sat a bunch of bananas. Not just a few loose bananas, but an entire branch that somebody had hacked off a banana tree, probably with a machete. I'm talking about 25 or so bananas bunched into several rows around the branch, all curled up like overgrown fingernails. Some were even green. Green fucking bananas! That's like kryptonite to an angler. For those of you who don't know, fishermen consider bananas on a boat extremely bad luck. This superstition applies to every kind of banana in every form — big, small, ripe, green. Banana bread and banana-nut muffins are delicious, but they have no place on a boat.

Various theories exist as to why fishermen consider bananas so awful. Back in the early days of the banana trade in the mid-1800s, crews would overload the banana boats when leaving the tropics. The boats would ride low in the water and often capsized in bad weather, leaving behind nothing but a chum slick of floating bananas. When the boats went missing, those who looked for the vessels found slicks of floating bananas that were miles long, so no one wanted to carry the fruit on board. Tons of spiders and bugs also made their way onto the boats in the banana crates. Crews would slip into their bunks and awake to creepy crawlies sliding up their thighs. Bugs found their way into the food supply on board and even in the crew's undergarments. No one escaped without multiple bites. All because of the damn bananas.

Hawaiians say bananas are bad luck because fishermen used to put them in their dugout canoes and head offshore. When the bananas started to rot, it marked the end of the fishing and time to go home. The Hawaiian gods felt you were being greedy if you had bananas on the boat and were also trying to catch fish. They would not bless your fishing trip.

Bananas also destroy other perishables. When bananas ripen, they release high volumes of ethylene gas, which is not only used as an anesthetic but also promotes the ripening of other fruits and vegetables. On long voyages this could ruin your food provisions and cause starvation among your crew. No matter how you look at this seemingly innocent fruit, it's just safer to leave them off the boat and keep the fish gods on your side.

"I think I know what you're doing wrong," I said to Enrico.

"What?" he asked.

I leapt to my feet and went right for him, jumping over the hi-low coffee table and closing the gap between us in astonishing fashion, especially when you consider my impaired physical state. My sudden movement surprised everyone, including myself.

Enrico instinctively lifted his arms to cover his head. I dove for the fruit and grabbed the banana stalk.

"This has no fucking place on a boat!" I yelled, holding the fruit above my head like the Incredible Hulk.

"But I am a banana farmer!" said Rafael.

I couldn't think of anything to say. I just flew into action, bolting for the salon door. I jetted out onto the cockpit and launched the bananas into the water like an Olympic javelin thrower. The oddly shaped branch was not very aerodynamic and it flew much like a drunken pelican, finally splashing down about 15 feet behind the boat.

"What was that?" Carlos hollered down from the bridge.

"Bananas!" I said. "We had a whole goddamn branch of bananas on this boat!"

The other men came out onto the deck, and we all watched the bananas float away into the distance. *Stupid, crazy American.*

Just as the yellow-and-green bananas began to dissolve into a pea-shaped speck on the horizon, the reel clicker on the left long went off, signaling that a big fish had just grabbed the bait. We were on. I lurched for the rod, pulled it out of the holder and reeled in the slack with the rod butt against my belly to make sure it was tight to the fish. Then I handed the rod to Rafael. A sailfish danced across the wake behind the boat, spraying water like a sprinkler.

"Forgive me," I said, "but don't ever bring bananas on a boat again."

CHAPTER FIVE

Down at Bud's

Virginia Key, Florida, circa 1981

You could drive down Rickenbacker Causeway and pass right by Bud's Fish Camp and never know it was there. People don't stumble in.

There are no signs, no traffic lights and no lit channel markers. Most folks looking for the Old Florida speakeasy zip right by the turn without even slowing down and end up back at the toll plaza on the causeway asking the cashier if he knows where the fish camp is. If he's in a good mood, the cashier may tell the driver where to turn. If the person behind the wheel happened to have a nice set of tits, the cashier may even waive the toll. If he's tired or cranky, the most common of all, the toll worker would just shrug his shoulders and go back to reading his paperback.

However, Bud's Fish Camp is worth turning around for. Bud's is the last stronghold for fishermen and their friends in the ever-gentrified land of misfits and malfeasance known as Miami. People fueled by the salty bounty of our Mother Ocean build joints like Bud's. People who understand that a cold beer tastes better after a long, shirtless day working in the sun will be sitting next to you. They may not look like you. They may not shower as often as you do. They may party more than you, but there is an unspoken bond that can be communicated in a brief gaze or head nod that says, 'I'm one of you.'

Tucked underneath a canopy of cedars, live oaks and unkempt cabbage palms on a small swath of land next to a water treatment facility on a little slice of easement in between the bright lights of Miami and the well-heeled mansions dotting the shores of Key Biscayne sits the cluster of buildings that forms Bud's Fish Camp.

On the surface, it's not a pretty place. A rusted-out school bus painted in a thousand different colors and splashed with graffiti has a massive rectangular cutout removed from its side with a stage extending outward made from recycled cinder blocks and wooden pallets. There's a beat-up mic and PA system. Anyone who wants to get up and shout, or strum and sing, is welcome. You'd be surprised at some of the musicians who cranked it up on this wobbly, not-quite-up-to-code soundstage. Sometimes Bud takes to the stage to recite his favorite poetry, or bang on a drum set created out of five-gallon buckets, circular saw blades and metal garbage-can lids. Eccentrics are welcomed.

Next to the bus is a tin-roof shed about the size of a mobile home. Made out of old reclaimed lumber and decorated with twinkle lights and fish mounts, this building gives Bud's the fish-camp feel. There are large windows with big plywood shutters that open vertically and clip to the roof. There are no screens because too many bottles and people have flown through them and Bud grew tired of replacing them. The sea breeze does a decent job of swatting away the mosquitoes and no-see-ums, and the smoke from the nearby fire pit helps keep unwanted critters at bay. The floor is plywood and a makeshift bar sits off to one side, but no one really sits at the bar. People mostly walk in and order a cold beer, guaranteed to be 32 degrees or colder, then step out into the gravel courtyard to sit down and enjoy the breeze and stars.

The patio furniture is a mishmash of colors and materials. Some days you might be sitting on an old stump, your elbows and drink resting on a giant wooden spool that once held telephone cable. Other days you may be kicked back in a hammock or melting into plastic furniture. Bud and his buddies regularly drive into Key Biscayne to pick through the trash left out by the millionaires. You'd be amazed at some of the treasures they've found over the years. Ceiling fans, hardly touched leather sofas, oriental rugs, picnic tables, brass beds, guitars, bicycles. Bud's favorite find is a wooden rocking chair. He's logged some serious time swaying back and forth on this chair, shooting the shit with shrimpers and strippers. The decor is ever evolving and always surprising.

The only air-conditioned room is Bud's office, a mobile unit that he won in a poker game from the head of a construction company. He even made the guy deliver it and set the structure on the edge of the camp. Bud planted native greenery all around his office, which flourished to the point where you could hardly see the trailer. The landscaping and vines around Bud's office grew so thick that he regularly cuts it back just to pull light in through the windows. His office is also his home, but no one says it outwardly because the place is not zoned for residential use. Bud's relationship with the city is an odd one, and there is no need to poke the bear. Slightly illegal things happen at Bud's that the cops know about but decide to ignore. Few people ever complain about the place, and Bud can be a very loud, squeaky hinge when he becomes unhinged.

While many come for the cold beer and to taste Bud's famous smoked fish dip — made from a mix of mullet and whiting, smoked over mesquite and mixed with onion, pimento cheese and celery — there are still plenty of true fishermen who pull up to Bud's. They often arrive by boat, at ungodly hours when there's nothing else open. They may buy a few dozen live shrimp and a pack of Marlboros at three in the morning. The place is just about always open, and if you can't find someone to scoop the shrimp out of the aerated tank, the net hangs right beside the gurgling water and there's a mason jar to stick your money in. "Help Yourself and Be Honorable | Shrimp $1.75/dozen," reads a sign. The price varies depending on the time of year, and so does the quality of the bait.

One dock runs alongside the land; it's more like a bulkhead. There are no finger docks, just the bulkhead and a row of pilings placed roughly 20 feet off of the dock. Boats back in, tie the bow off to the pilings and fasten the stern to the dock. The tide can really rip here so they use at least one spring line off each side of the boat to keep the vessel situated right in between the pilings and not rubbing against one side or the other.

The boats that dock at Bud's aren't going to win any beauty contests. They're work boats. Built for a purpose. Hauling stone-crab traps, netting pompano or trawling for shrimp. There isn't much depth at Bud's, so nothing over 25 feet docks here.

The owners of these vessels are not rich men. They're working men and they choose to work on the water. They have good seasons and bad ones. Their businesses are at Mother Nature's mercy. And the fact that they tie up next to a bar puts a damper on their take-home, but they wouldn't have it any other way. Bud looks out for them but has had to throw the hammer down on many occasions. You can only be nice for so long. At some point you become a target, and when Bud is finished with you, that's it. You get thrown out with the trash.

Bud stays in constant motion. His frenetic energy helps him burn a lot of calories, and he maintains a slight frame despite a penchant for frozen strawberry daiquiris, which he jazzes up with vanilla ice cream. His vision is horrible, and he wears thick, gold-framed glasses that often slip down his squat Greek nose. He first looks at you over the top of the frames, then cocks his head back to see the in-focus version. For some of his customers, the soft-blurred vision is preferred. The glasses have a beaded chain that runs around his neck should they completely fall off. He cuts his own hair and has done so since his twenties. It's a simple cut. Utilitarian. Around the ears, brushed back on top with some hair cream, and runs about halfway down the back of his neck. He must be close to 60 now, though you really wouldn't know it other than the crow's feet scratching at his temples and the gray hair on his head and chest.

Bud is shirtless from 10 in the morning till four in the afternoon. His skin is beyond tanned; it is the color of mahogany, a rich, dark reddish-brown mahogany stretched out like cured deer hide. He showers at dusk and then puts on a plain white T-shirt and a pair of blue Dickies pants held up with black suspenders. Once in a while he busts out a guayabera shirt on a Saturday night, but his usual uniform consists of a plain white tee that has yellowed under the arms and around the neck. He wears boat shoes and no socks. Never socks. Bud looks like he could either be homeless or an eccentric millionaire. It's typically a fine line. And he likes to leave people guessing. He can easily hold a conversation with a bankrupt crabber or the CEO of a Fortune 500 company. Bud reads the newspaper every morning and is a wealth of knowledge when it comes to nature and biology. He can name every plant, fish, reptile or bird that lives in South Florida. He can also wax on and on about the corrupt politicians, sugar plantations and the habitat destruction of his beloved Everglades.

Bud obtained the rights to build his fish camp on this stretch of county-owned property in the late 1950s when the Knight brothers were looking for land to construct a new home for the *Miami Herald*. Bud owned a small marina and fishing pier right at the end of 15th Street in Miami, which just so happened to be the perfect spot for the *Herald*'s new state-of-the-art fortress/headquarters built to withstand Category Four hurricanes, thick with concrete and fueled with backup power to keep the presses running in triple-digit-speed winds and syndicate stories.

Bud wasn't opposed to selling out. He liked the newspaper's owner, Jack Knight, and respected his tenacity and aggressive, accurate reporting style that helped the *Herald* thrive after a somewhat unfruitful start. Bud wasn't exactly a downtown kind of guy anyhow. The men agreed to a handsome buyout, which eliminated all of Bud's debt and put a decent amount of money into his bank account. But before signing anything Bud requested some land to build more docks for his customers, the fishermen who tied up their boats with him, bought his food and tackle, and swapped tales into the wee hours. Jack Knight used his connections with the city and county to persuade them to designate a small, half-acre plot of land on Virginia Key, right on the water, for Bud's new camp.

Virginia Key served as a 'colored' beach during the days of segregation. From the 1940s through the 1960s, African Americans and the darker Latin inhabitants were not allowed to enter the Atlantic Ocean from the shores of Miami's swank South Beach. The city leaders struck a deal with the black community and designated Virginia Key as the "colored" beach. But there was no bridge at the time. To get back and forth to the island for picnics and swimming, beach-goers had to bum rides from local fishermen, and many of the boats at Bud's dock were more than happy to bring folks over and pick them up for a little fee. Bud knew the area well and was pleased to stake his claim on Virginia Key. He moved in sometime in the early 1960s and never looked back, continually improving the place, adding seating and docks as he could afford. He dodged storms — political and tropical — often riding them out. Bud maintained an open-door policy. Anyone was welcome, just don't be an asshole.

Joe McPhee first wandered into Bud's some 20 years after Bud opened the doors. Joe had set up a satellite office in South Florida and purchased an 18-foot skiff that he kept on Virginia Key. He could afford to put his boat in a marina on Miami Beach, but he liked the folks who hung out at Bud's. He tried to glean as much info as he could from the shrimpers and crabbers about the inlets, deep channels and bait-fishing spots. Learning the local waters helped him find and catch tarpon, his new favorite quarry.

"Who's the kid?" Joe asked Bud, motioning with his chin toward a young shrimper who was cleaning up his boat, scrubbing on his hands and knees. This particular shrimp boat was freshly painted, its nets tied up neatly, baskets new, and all of the lines holding it to the dock were bright white. All of the other vessels were floating rust stains, Mickey Mouse crafts held together with makeshift cuts of plywood, zip ties and 5200 marine sealant.

Bud looked over the top of his glasses, squinting a bit. "Oh, that's Jensi," he said. "Good kid, pays me on time. Never comes home with an empty boat."

"Yen-see?"

"Yeah, I dunno how you spell it, but that's his name, Jensi," Bud said. "He's a Cuban kid. His folks are good people. They come over here and fish with him sometimes. He's fished this bay for years. He used to ride his bike down all of the causeways at night scooping shrimp with a long-handled net he made out of a closet rod. He'd go to school smelling like a bucket of bait, but the fucking kid loved it."

Joe nodded his head, intrigued. Joe didn't realize it at the time, but he was shopping around for a fishing partner. He'd gone fishing with a few guys he met through his business dealings in Florida, but none stuck. Good fishing partners must mirror each other when it comes to desire, work ethic and knowledge base. If you have one person who knows much more than the other, the balance of the boat goes off kilter and one man ends up doing most of the work simply because he knows more. This is acceptable as long as the man with less knowledge picks things up quickly and improves his game to restore the balance. But, if he lets the stronger angler continually overcompensate for his lacking abilities, well, then you have the start of an ugly situation.

Then there's work ethic. If both men decide that the boat will leave at five in the morning and one man doesn't arrive until quarter to six, and shows zero remorse for his tardiness, don't bother inviting him back. Unless someone died or you ended up in jail, there shall be no running late to go fishing. The same goes for pitching in on the boat. Thou shalt not sleep all day. The same must be said for helping out back at the dock: Filleting fish, cleaning the boat, turning wrenches in the engine room and swabbing the head are not above or below any man. Do your part.

Let's not forget about the subject of booze. Many guys use fishing as an excuse to sit on a piece of fiberglass and pop tops all day. Surely there's nothing wrong with that, unless you're in a boat with a man driven more by the passion of chasing fish than the desire to fall down drunk. If both guys are there jointly to catch a buzz rather than catch fish, then there is no problem. If one guy is more of a purist angler, say hello to big problems. Even massive yachts become small little places when you're trying to hide from someone else on board.

Finding a good fishing partner is like finding a mate in life. You have to mesh and become one — a tighter unit together than apart. If you find that person, hold on with two hands because you will embark on adventures greater than anything you ever dreamt up. But you will undoubtedly have to weed through some shitty partners before finding the right fit.

Joe's ongoing search had taken him on countless dreadful journeys, but he never gave up hope. Not when a supposed fishing partner ran Joe's boat aground after professing knowledge in piloting all types of vessels, big and small. Not when a potential suitor lost not one but two of Joe's custom-built rod-and-reel combos over the side of the boat in a single day. Not when a granny knot let go of a potential world record just two seconds after coming tight. Not when the drain plug failed to make it into the transom, leading to Joe's most embarrassing trip to the launch ramp ever.

There were many such bad matches in Joe's past, and he had become more adept at sniffing out the lackeys and focusing on the core traits that he thought made a good angler. In Joe's mind, a good captain notes all of the conditions all of the time. He can tell you the exact moon phase the last time the fish bit. He can tell you how many times a certain lure got hit versus another lure. He can describe the currents and knows what part of the tide is best for each species.

A good captain also takes care of his vessel as if it were his favorite child. Baby the boat — don't run it at full throttle just because you can. Take care of your vessel, and your tackle, and they will take care of you. And finally, be a man of honor. If you say you're going to do something, then fucking do it!

Joe walked toward Jensi's boat with two cold beers and offered one to the young captain. Jensi was wearing navy mechanic's pants that had been faded by the sun to a light sky blue. His once-white, long-sleeve, button-down collared shirt was stained around the torso from bait and blood, faded, thin and looked very soft from a million or so washes. The young man rolled the sleeves up to his elbows, revealing his tanned, wiry forearms and calloused hands. He had a deck brush in one hand and a hose in the other. The boat was maybe 20 feet with outriggers on each side that operated the wing nets used to drag for shrimp in the bay. Unlike some of the other boats that docked at Bud's, Jensi's rig had a fairly large cockpit. It was almost all deck space in fact, and more of an open boat with a small helm and windshield far forward near the point of the bow. There was no cabin to speak of. No way to get out of bad weather other than a set of slickers. Jensi operated his boat alone, driving it, setting the nets, hauling gear and sorting his catch. Each outrigger held one end of a wing net. The net extended from each side of the boat and culminated in a ring-shaped holding segment that formed a long tube behind the vessel. He targeted pink shrimp, which push out of the estuaries into Biscayne Bay and its nearby passes and channels as water cools. The shrimp run strongest during the cooler months, from December through April, or thereabouts. The best time to trawl for them is during an outgoing tide as the current pulls the shrimp out of the shallower brackish areas into the deeper bay.

Jensi started in the business by scooping shrimp from the local piers and bridges with a net he'd made by fastening two wooden closet rods together. It was about 15 feet long so he could hover it deep into the moving current and pull up any shrimp flying by. The net he attached to the end was deep bodied so he could scoop 70 or more shrimps without having to haul the heavy net up and dump out his prize. As a kid, he struggled to pull the big net in, hand over hand. Over time his skinny arms grew strong. Defined biceps emerged and his back became wide like a swimmer's. Jensi's mother would drop him off after school and he'd work Venetian Causeway, Bear Cut and Rickenbacker Causeway until he filled two or three five-gallon buckets full of shrimp. He'd call his mother to pick him up in her station wagon. He laid plastic down in the storage area by the hatchback. The plastic kept any water off the carpet, but it couldn't hide the smell. She never complained. They'd sell the shrimp to some of the restaurants in Little Havana, or fry them up and make pressed sandwiches with fresh Cuban bread, lime and spicy mayo. The neighbors would line up to purchase a sandwich, often after church. Jensi saved his money, and at the age of 16, he bought his first boat.

"Buy you a beer?" Joe asked, holding out one of the beers by its neck.

"Sure," Jensi said. "Thanks."

"You bet. I don't want to sound like a pervert or something, but I've watched you come in the last couple of nights and you always have more shrimp than these other guys. Why is that?" Joe asked.

Jensi took a long pull on the cold beer, wondering what was up with this guy. Jensi noticed Joe's expensive watch and clean fingernails. Two things he didn't often see at Bud's. "I just fish a little harder," he said.

Joe nodded. "Listen, I don't know anything about catching shrimp, but I'm really in love with catching a species that likes to *eat* shrimp. So, I'm wondering, do you see a lot of tarpon when you're out there at night?"

"How many is a lot?" Jensi asked, smiling.

"I'll take that as a yes," Joe said and extended his hand. "My name is Joe McPhee. I just started spending more time here in Miami and haven't been able to really dial in the tarpon fishery. I bought a skiff and wonder if you might join me sometime and show me some of the spots where you've seen tarpon."

Jensi took another pull on the beer. He sees tarpon on just about every trip. They may be hiding in the shadows of a bridge, waiting to pounce on bait, rolling in the Cut or busting schools of finger mullet off the beaches. He always had a fondness for tarpon, the speed and agility they could muster out of their long, slender bodies. But there was no market for tarpon. They spooked shrimp, and if one got in his net, it would cost him a lengthy repair. So Jensi often stayed away from them, but it had been awhile since he went sport fishing with a rod and reel.

"There's no money in tarpon fishing," Jensi said. "I have bills to pay."

"I'd disagree with that one. The guides on Biscayne Bay get paid a nice daily rate to take customers out and put them on tarpon and bonefish. I'd be more than happy to pay you if you'll guide me on my boat."

Sport fishing and some money for his wallet ... Jensi reached out his hand and Joe took it.

"You've got a deal," Jensi said.

CHAPTER SIX

Square Grouper

T he heat from the midday sun felt like molten magma on what little exposed skin on my body was left open to the elements. When fishing the flats there is no shade whatsoever on the boat. Nowhere to hide. To combat the evil rays of Helios, I wore a long-sleeve shirt, a wide-brimmed hat, full-length, feather-weight pants and a neck gaiter. The light fabrics blocked the sun and kept it from frying most of my skin. Polarized sunglasses protected my retinas from the brutal glare bouncing off the water and the deck of the boat. They also let me see through the waves, to spot fish and the countless lifeforms that thrive in the shallow water of Florida Bay. Gray snapper, pinfish, crabs, mullet — every day, every hour, the scenery changed with each push of the boat over a grass flat. I also wore light angling gloves to curb the deterioration of the skin on my fingers as I stripped line to move the fly through the water, or held tightly against the pull of the meanest, most graceful, powerful fish that lives in this environment. The only part of my body completely unprotected, except for a heavy slathering of 70-proof sunblock, are my feet. I can't wear shoes when fly-fishing from a casting deck. I've tried, and I will bring shoes, but when I'm casting I prefer to be barefoot so I can feel the line if it gets wrapped around a toe or ankle. Then I can hop out of a tangle and hopefully avoid one of a million or so pitfalls that can undo a spectacular catch.

The wind had died out hours earlier, and the late-July beat-down from the heavens sabotaged whatever little energy I had left. I was broken. I had just lost my second hooked tarpon of the day. We had jumped several more but only got two hooks to stick. I fought the 70-pounder with all of the strength my body could muster. My gut was sore from jamming the butt of the fly rod into my soft flesh. My hands ached. My back pounded. The bottoms of my feet felt like sandpaper. My mind had turned to fire, angry that the fish had won. But it didn't matter; the great silver king had made mincemeat out of me. It ran like a thoroughbred. Shook its head like an enraged bronco. Launched its entire body four or five feet out of the water in a desperate attempt to spit the hook, but that didn't end the battle. The fight ended when the wide-eyed beast charged the boat and bolted right under the hull. I didn't have much time to react. I shoved the rod into the water, but the old king knew what he was doing. The fish made a left turn around the skeg of the outboard motor, that little metal keel just below the propeller, and snapped us off. Just one of those days.

Jensi didn't say a word. He didn't have to. I could read his face. His pursed lips, lack of eye contact and deep sigh said enough. He was just as upset as I was, maybe more so, but I knew he wouldn't say anything about it. I'm sure he felt he should've pushed the boat backward with his long push pole to escape the charging tarpon. We were in the shallows. Not enough water to start the engine. All movement of the vessel relied on Jensi's push pole, of which he was a master maneuverer. He could push a boat straight and true in a 20-knot crosswind. His balance never wavered on the poling platform, standing firm above the outboard on a two-foot-by-two-foot slab of nonskid fiberglass. Even at 64 years old, he poled a boat better than any man I'd ever known. I wouldn't want to fish the flats with any other person, except Daddy.

"You need a break?" he asked me.

I nodded my head. "Let's go find some shade," I said.

Jensi pushed the boat into an unmarked channel with deep enough water for him to start the engine and motor us to a sun shelter he knew.

The 18-foot flats skiff popped up on plane and zipped across the still waters like a low-flying gull. Jensi never ran the boat wide open, preferring to run at a smooth 25 mph or so. At this speed the wind dried off the sweat on my forehead, replenishing my tank some. I took off my hat and sunglasses, closing my eyes to the moving air, a wind-filled shower for my broken spirit. I was sitting on the padded livewell just in front of the center console where Jensi was steering the boat. He put his arm around my neck lightly and leaned in, laying his head on my shoulder so I could hear him

71

speak.

"We'll find plenty more fish, Parker. You know that. You didn't do anything wrong," he said and tussled my hair.

It was everything I needed to hear.

The dark-black plastic wrapping would've completely concealed the package were I not crouching just a few feet from it. It was about the size of a microwave oven and nearly the same shape.

"Is that what I think it is?" I asked.

"I sure hope not," Jensi responded. "Don't touch it, Parker. Let's get out of here."

Jensi, my lifelong tarpon guide, began to slide the skiff backward, pulling on a buttonwood tree branch. He had pushed the boat into a little creek in the mangroves, seeking some shade for a short regrouping. The July sun on the Florida Bay flats had sucked us dry, devoid of life. We needed a reprieve from the heat and glare. A chance to cool off, down some fluids and snack on Mami's leftover fried chicken. An intermission. We were too far from the house to head back for lunch like we normally do.

I had just lost a battle with a large tarpon that I'd managed to hook on my 12-weight Sage fly rod. The battle took more than an hour, and if we left now to go home, we would miss the sunset bite. We never missed the sunset bite, unless the wind blew a gale.

I put up my hand. "Not so fast," I said. "I just want to take a look. I've never seen one. I mean I've heard about them. We've all heard about them, but I've never seen one in real life."

"Whoever lost that thing is probably looking for it," Jensi said sternly. "I don't need those types of people showing up here. Neither do you!"

I didn't listen. I moved to the tip of the bow, lying on my belly with an outstretched hand. I could barely place my fingertips on the bumpy black plastic rectangle, the top of my head scratching on the branch of a red mangrove dotted with barnacles and white growth. I kept stretching with one hand and held onto the bow with my other. The tips of my fingers slid across the thick black plastic. It was smooth to the touch but hard when I pushed against it. Solid. A brick of something illegal. Cannabis? Cocaine? The curiosity quickly built up inside my mind until I was yanked backward by my ankles. My chin slammed into the rub rail on the edge of the skiff's gunwale.

"What the hell, Jensi!" I yelled.

"Shut up, Parker! We're getting out of here before we get ourselves in too deep."

I often refer to Jensi as my Cuban papi. He's known me since I was in diapers. He has been the most permanent figure in my life. Jensi and his wife, whom I've always just called Mami, are like my grandparents. They practically raised me. Jensi taught me to value the gifts I've been given, and how to care for things like boats, cars, homes and personal relationships. Rich kids tend to lack an appreciation for things and disregard how hard most people have to work to afford them. Jensi made sure I didn't fall into that category.

Jensi did much to make me into a man, even though I often fail at being a good one. All these years, all the fucked-up shit I had done, and Jensi never laid a hand on me, even when I lit his shoes on fire, or wrecked his truck. He always forgave me, and never walked away from me. But he never put up with my bullshit either.

I always knew when I did something wrong on the boat because he would clang his gold wedding band against the stainless-steel steering wheel. That sound would stop me in my tracks and I'd look back at him to read his face. To this day, I freeze up when I hear that clang of metal on metal.

If I really fucked up, he'd discipline me by making me scrape barnacles off of a boat for days. Or I'd have to clean and devein hundreds of pounds of shrimp. He was my Mr. Miyagi, but he spoke Spanish. I replaced and greased bearings, put on countless coats of wax, deboned mullet, pressure-watched stone-crab traps. The punishments varied depending on the severity of the crime and what kind of work needed to be done around the house. I always did the work, but I often complained about it. I knew that if I didn't do what Jensi wanted, he wouldn't take me fishing. That was the worst punishment of all.

Whenever I do something stupid or find myself in trouble, it's never Daddy's reaction that I care most about. I wonder what Jensi would think of me. I've always measured my actions by Jensi's reaction. He is not an overly emotional person, but I know Jensi loves me. I know because he never says no when I need help. He is completely reliable. Unconditional reliability. He isn't super affectionate, but he always finds a way to pat my shoulder, throw his hand around my neck or rub my head with his ropelike, calloused hands. I'm the closest thing to a son Jensi and Mami have in their lives. We've spent many holidays together, but nearly all of our bonding has occurred during the Florida Keys' tarpon season.

Since I was a pre-teen I'd spent most of late spring and early summer in the Florida Keys with Jensi and Mami. Daddy would pop in from time to time as he could, but he sent me down for the duration. It was my form of summer camp, minus the girls. Daddy had bought a place on Tavernier Creek and hired Jensi to take care of the property and the boats and guide us for tarpon season. After tarpon season was over, Jensi fished on other boats for other species. He bottom-fished and spear-dived for yellowtail snapper and grouper. He occasionally went offshore for mahimahi. He caught pinfish, mullet and pilchards and sold them to bait shops. Daddy paid Jensi a decent salary and he didn't have to fish for the money. He had to fish for his soul.

When I was 10 I caught a 40-pound barracuda on 12-pound-test line fishing with Jensi and Daddy on the edge of Snake Creek. It was the largest fish I had ever caught at the time. At one point the 'cuda had nearly peeled all of the line off the reel and Daddy reached for the rod, but Jensi wouldn't let him. He wanted me to use the skills he had taught me. I let the fish take line when it kicked its tail and sped off like a thieving cat. I reeled in line when I could and maintained tension on the animal throughout the fight.

I caught the fish entirely on my own and when Jensi grabbed the tail of the three-foot-long gnarly toothed creature and brought it on board, I went crazy, jumping up and down and climbing all over Daddy. You couldn't contain my excitement. We took photos with a small 35 mm camera that Jensi kept on the boat back then. Jensi set the timer on the camera and perched it on the poling platform, using a rag to keep it in place. The three of us stood in a line on the bow of the boat, me in the middle, with the fish. I couldn't hold the fish by myself. Jensi held the head to keep me safely away from the half-inch fangs while I cupped the 'cuda's midsection and Daddy grasped the tail. We released the fish, but the joy and exhilaration stayed with me for several months.

When my birthday came around later that year, I received a package from Jensi. In a handwritten letter, he described every detail of that day, recounting the weather conditions, the state of the tide, how much line the fish took, and the length and girth measurements of the barracuda. He told me how proud he was of me, calling me a "true sportsman." He constructed a frame out of an old lobster pot for an 8-by-10 photo of the three of us with the big 'cuda. Below the photo he mounted the lure I had used to catch the fish. The lure was ravaged. The 'cuda's fang-like teeth notched the sides of the wooden lure and removed chunks of white and pink paint. War wounds. I had completely forgotten what lure I had used to catch the fish, but Jensi kept it. Jensi remembered everything. I taped his letter to the back of the frame, and when I'm feeling defeated, I flip it around and read his words. I don't know what it cost him to make this gift for me, but it is perhaps the most valuable thing I own.

Daddy first met Jensi before I was born on one of his many business trips to Miami. Daddy had real estate in South Florida and had opened a machine shop in Homestead. The cost of labor was low, as were property taxes, and the location gave him access to a burgeoning agriculture industry. Miami became the official gateway to the Caribbean, Central America and beyond. The shop grew quickly and there were always containers of all sorts of equipment getting sent to the port for destinations abroad. This growing business also gave Daddy an excuse to spend more time in the Sunshine State, especially during the winter months.

"Your dad and I didn't know much about tarpon fishing when we first started," Jensi recalled. "I knew a lot of spots in Biscayne Bay, and your dad knew the tackle. In the beginning we fished with live bait most of the time. Shrimp or pilchards, maybe crabs. To me, it was very educational. I had never driven a skiff or poled a boat. We just learned by doing. And we got pretty good at it."

The pair fished the bridges at night or along the breakwall in Government Cut, if the boat traffic wasn't unbearable in the small skiff.

Tarpon will destroy tackle like an elephant stomping on a paper cup. If there is any weakness in the gear, a tarpon will find it. A bad knot will slip. A chafed line will snap. A cheap hook will straighten out. Daddy broke off his fair share of fish, and each time it happened he made mental notes so he could change up his presentation or beef up his tackle so it wouldn't happen again. Jensi focused on learning the locations, the tides and conditions that influenced the bite. He learned how to sneak up on fish so they wouldn't spook, giving Daddy a good angle to cast a bait or maybe a lure. Jensi mastered the art of poling a skiff. He also perfected his ability to spot fish in the water, a skill that is more valuable than any bit of marine electronics or fishing gear.

Every once in a while, Daddy would send me a few photos and a letter when I was at school: "Caught six tarpon today. Jensi spotted them from 60 yards and we got them to eat. Lost two. Going to put you on some fish when you get here. Love, Daddy."

The photos would show the big animals leaping into the air, throwing white water like a raging river rapid, the fish's gills open as it shook its big head atop the long, silvery body. I saved all of the photos and showed them to my buddies and teachers, bragging about my upcoming trips once school ended.

Daddy and Jensi meshed into the ideal fishing team. Equally adept at their roles. Together they excelled and it fueled their desire to fish more. Nighttime expeditions worked better for Daddy's schedule. Meetings and work in the day, maybe a short nap and some food, and then fishing from eight to two, unless the tides were shit. Their friendship also blossomed, a mutual respect planted firmly in both of them. Jensi would listen to Daddy's tips on managing money and the importance of building his savings and purchasing property.

Daddy loved Jensi's ability to fix anything with practically no tools and no materials.

"Cuban mechanics are the best in the world," Daddy would tell me with affection in his voice, not sarcasm. "They can fix an outboard with nothing more than a rubber band and some chewing gum." That last part being sarcasm, of course.

Jensi inherited his father's abilities to diagnose complicated mechanical systems and fix them very simply. It's impossible to find parts for anything in Cuba, so you have to be inventive and find ways to make things work. Jensi hated to throw things away. He'd tinker with toasters and lawn mowers that others had given up on. Nine times out of 10 he got it working better than it ever had. If it was a lost cause, he'd harvest whatever salvageable parts he could and save them for the next project.

"I had a refrigerator in my condo that kept going out on me," Daddy said. "The thing was a total piece of crap, and I kept having to toss my frozen fish and steaks. It was driving me crazy. I mentioned it to Jensi on the boat one day and told him what it was doing. He knew exactly what was wrong. He came over the next day and rewired the whole unit. I mean, he was soldering wires together on this little motherboard. I have no idea what he did, but it worked better than the day I bought the place and it never went out again. Cuban mechanics, man. They're fucking magicians."

After they mastered fishing for tarpon with bait, they started to fish lures and artificials, enjoying the added challenge. Switching to plugs also helped them cut down on time spent fishing for bait, allowing them to spend more time on tarpon. Top-water lures were Daddy's favorite. Getting the attention of a big tarpon with a chugger pushing water on the surface elicited some of the most dramatic takes he'd ever seen of any fish. Tarpon don't just snatch a lure; they engulf it, leaving nothing but a big hole in the water where the lure once was. Daddy loved fishing lures, and bait for that matter; he didn't really care which technique they used and they often had a bit of everything on the boat. But when he got into fly-fishing for tarpon, Daddy dove in big time and took Jensi with him. Within a few months, the condo in Miami looked more like a fly shop than a two-bedroom unit in a high-rise. The dining-room table became a fly-tying workbench. The armoire in the living room was bursting with chicken feathers, hooks, flashabou, and plastic bags filled with Mylar and thread. Jensi loved it too.

Fly-tying suited Jensi's Cuban magicianry. He created flies that resembled little green crabs, with bouncy eyes and dangling legs. Jensi was a fly-tyer more out of necessity. He didn't like buying bucktail material or feathers. He used Daddy's stuff, but he really enjoyed making flies out of odds and ends he found around the house. He used yarn and flashy colors from sweaters he found at thrift shops that he would pull apart. He cut vinyl into tiny strips for flash and made his own eyeballs out of beads and magic marker. Some of his creations were true masterpieces so closely resembling the real thing that he fooled the boatyard cats down at Bud's, where he would have them running around the docks, chasing a hookless fuzz ball. He also liked to tease Mami. He once tied a black crab pattern that looked a lot like a big fat spider. He attached the hairy spider to a 12-inch piece of light fishing line, and what he did next nearly got him divorced. He attached the spider to the back of Mami's favorite house coat. When she put the coat on and saw that artificial spider, she screamed, ran across the house, arms flailing like someone on fire. The worst part was, the spider was following her, bouncing around on the fishing line as if it were jumping on her back over and over. She finally ripped the coat off and beat the black blob with the heel of her shoe. After about 20 good smacks, she figured out what had happened and spotted Jensi on his knees, laughing uncontrollably, hands slapping the ground with vigor. She went after him with her shoe next.

Jensi and Daddy took to fly-casting, especially Daddy. He could throw a 12-weight all day, effortlessly dropping flies 60 or 70 feet. His presentation was perfect. The cast would unroll like a swell on the beach, gently plopping the fly down with very little disturbance. He'd zip shrimp patterns up under the mangroves. He could get a fly to land softly under a dock. He was a sharp shooter. He learned to combat the wind, a fly-fisherman's biggest foe, by casting with the wind, and then punching the fly behind him directly into it. Sometimes the move failed, sending the fly into his cap, but most times it worked.

Daddy taught me to fly-fish on the forward deck of his skiff. He'd stand behind me, one hand on my lower back, and the other holding my right arm as I worked the fly rod.

"You don't need to whip it. Focus on the motion and get your rhythm," he said. "Go from two o'clock to 10 o'clock. Load the rod. Be fluid. Not too many false casts. Now let the fly go."

He was surprisingly patient with me when it came to fly-fishing. I think it's because he viewed throwing a fly more as art than tossing bait, which is more about putting fish in the box and a fillet on the plate. Fly-fishing is different than conventional angling in that way. Fly-fishermen may travel to some little island in the Caribbean, fish for days, catch one nice fish on a flawless cast and call it the best trip of his life. For fly guys, it's not about numbers. It's about putting your time in. Immersing yourself in the environment and touching every element of the fishery. Overcoming any calamity that could possibly come your way. Breakoffs. Bad weather. Uncooperative fish. If they fished through all the adversity and finally made the perfect cast at the perfect time — stripped the fly just right to pull in a big bonefish or the holy grail, the ever-discriminating permit — and got that fish to bite and stay on the hook, well then that was an epic trip. Fly-fishermen are more glass half-full that way. I'm a bit fly-fisherman but I'm still a bit of a bait dunker as well. Unlike those snooty permit, I don't discriminate. I may even toss a crab at that permit, so it better be ready.

"There are certain fish that were built perfectly for fly-fishing," Daddy said. "Tarpon and bonefish because they live in the shallows and feed on small bitty baits. They are beautiful, their environments are idyllic and you can just walk a flat with a fly rod to catch them. That's perfect. Trout too. You just can't mimic a trout's diet better than a fly. I mean they eat fucking bugs!"

Daddy eventually moved his tarpon operation south to the Florida Keys. He purchased a lot on Tavernier Creek, with a dock, a boat lift and a small two-bedroom house. He fixed up the existing house and built a larger dwelling, constructed on 15-foot pilings so the house was a story and a half off the ground. This protected it from any storm surge, and the area below the house was perfect for parking boats on trailers. Daddy bought a new flats boat, the best one money could buy, and shipped a 22-foot center console down from up north. Jensi was put on the payroll, and he and Mami moved into the two-bedroom cottage. Jensi watched after the houses, the yard, the dock, the vehicles, the boats and anything with a motor, while Mami took care of life inside the houses and her men as she liked to call us. She cooked our meals, washed our clothes, cleaned the house and kept us out of trouble. This was to become my one true home.

Nine months out of the year I would find myself in a different boarding school or in a new room with some rich-kid roommate. School and I got along as well as a warden and an inmate. I couldn't wait to get out and head to the Keys for tarpon season. In the Keys, I found structure. I had Mami's food and motherly touch. She was always doing extra things for me. Small things, like sneaking me homemade cookies or staying in my room and rubbing my back till I fell asleep if I wasn't feeling well. She never yelled at me. She only showed me love. Unconditional love. Motherly love that my life had been stripped of. We'd sit on the couch together watching movies or playing cards. We danced to her favorite show tunes and she'd attempt to teach me Latin dances like the merengue. I spent time with her in the kitchen, learning to cook ropa vieja and yucca. I was the only Irish kid at my boarding school who knew what lechon asado was and could actually execute it, marinating the pork shoulder in mojo sauce for a day and cooking it slowly over charcoal.

The fishing fell into a routine. Wake up about 5:30 a.m., have breakfast and look at the weather and tide charts to come up with a plan as to where we'd start the day. Pack a cooler. Take inventory of fishing tackle. Hit the water as the sun was ascending over the ocean. Fish the morning bite and run back to the house for lunch and some downtime. Leave the house again around four in the afternoon for the sunset bite. Back to the house around eight.

Clean the boat and tackle. Shower. Eat dinner. Tie flies till we passed out. Wake up and do it again. Rinse, wash, repeat.

This lasted for a good two months or so. Sometimes we'd mix it up and take the center console offshore to catch mahimahi or kingfish. Jensi was also an expert snapper fisherman and we'd go out at night to load the freezer with yellowtail.

The tarpon moved and we moved with them. The conditions changed. The water changed. We were always adapting to improve our success. The fish kept us guessing.

"I just want to see what's in it," I said to Jensi, reaching up to grab a mangrove branch to hold the boat in place as I shifted around. Jensi was 40 years older than me and ripped, but I outweighed him by a good 50 pounds. The tug-of-war didn't last long. He picked up the push pole and swung it at me, whacking me on the shoulder. Hard.

"What the fuck, man?! Are you crazy?" I yelled.

"Me? No, you're the fucking crazy one!" he screamed back. "This is not a debate, Parker. We are getting out of here. This is no joke."

"We haven't seen but two boats all morning. They were skiffs. Flats boats, Jensi. No one but Mami has any idea where we are. Let's chill out for a minute. This is nothing to freak out about."

He shook his head and sat down behind the console. I could see he was pissed.

"I'm just curious, Jensi. Aren't you a little bit curious?"

"Of course I am, but I'm not an idiot. It's drugs. I don't give a shit what kind of drugs. Drugs are drugs. I don't want whatever is in that thing and I don't want you to have them. So why are we sitting here even talking about it? Someone dropped that in the bay. We found it by accident and we're going to leave it right where we found it."

"You're such a party pooper," I said and turned around to crawl back toward the plastic bail.

"Parker, I'm warning you. You put that thing on this boat and we will have a major problem on our hands."

I ignored him and got my hands on the package again. It was wedged in between the mangrove roots pretty tightly. I yanked on it and shoved it from side to side. It began to free up.

"Parker, stop!"

I didn't turn around.

"Parker! Look at me, goddamnit."

The boat was sliding back out of the little creek. Jensi was pulling us out.

"Hey!" I said. "This is my boat, and I want to see what this thing is. Maybe we report it to the cops or something. But don't move this boat, Jensi. Don't forget who works for who here."

"You really want to pull that shit with me right now, young man?" he said in a very scary tone.

I had hit the dickhead button and Jensi wasn't backing down.

He turned around, his head facing the stern of the boat, opened a hatch and began digging around for something.

"What are you going to do?" I said in a sort of threatening way. My eyes telling him I wasn't scared.

Jensi pulled out a small speargun that he used when diving for hogfish. He pointed it at me.

"Don't make me do it," he said.

"Do what? Shoot me? You're going to fucking shoot me with a speargun? Gimme a break." I laughed a little. There's no way he would do it, I thought, and I turned back toward the bail of Acapulco gold.

"Last warning," Jensi said. I ignored him. I grabbed the bail and yanked it free from the timbers. It was heavier than I figured, probably waterlogged. I struggled to lift it from my position — I was lying on my belly on the forward deck of the boat. I had no leverage. Using all the strength in my core I had left after battling those fish, I somehow swung the bail into the boat. As I turned my head in triumph, Jensi pulled the trigger. The spear released in a flash, zipping into the side of my ass with a thud. A shot of white-lightning pain flashed through my entire body. Hot, fierce pain like I'd been stabbed. I screamed so loudly that all of the birds in the mangroves flushed out in one large mass of feathery movement.

"You shot me!" I yelled, rolling around on the deck. "You fucking shot me!"

"You're a dumbass, Parker!" he hollered, quickly pushing the mystery bail back into the water with his foot. He pulled on the mangroves to slide the boat out of the creek. "I told you not to touch it! Why didn't you listen to me, you little shit?"

The pain made me nauseous. The spear had gone into the edge of my butt cheek, the tip of it pushing against the skin on the other side. Surprisingly, there wasn't much blood.

"I'm going to fire you!" I yelled. "You hear me, you're fucking fired! And Mami is going to kill you! You're a fucking sociopath, Jensi. You shot me! My God, I can't believe you fucking shot me. And it fucking hurts!"

I was crying and had curled one leg into the fetal position on the deck of the boat. My injured leg remained straight.

"It's not that bad," he said. "I'm sorry. Let's go home. We might need to get you a tetanus shot."

I didn't fire Jensi. I figured if he would shoot me, imagine what he'd do to everyone else.

CHAPTER SEVEN

The Toilet Paper King's Mighty Sword

"Well, well, well, if it isn't Parker McPhee," said Capt. John Randall, half smiling as I walked up the ladder to the boat's flybridge and sat down on the settee in front of him.

"Good to see you, Cappy," I said.

John was at the helm, plugging some numbers into his GPS chartplotter and poring over his logbooks. The boat, a 58-foot custom-built offshore machine constructed by a well-respected New Zealand builder, looked immaculate. Most charter boats resemble war-torn PT boats, full of cracked gelcoat and blotchy red rust stains. Not John's boat.

He used only the best possible equipment you could find. Cost? It didn't matter. He cared only about craftsmanship and longevity. When it came to the boat or fishing the deep waters of the South Pacific, he didn't buy things for flash. He bought only equipment he could rely on. He was taking men out to fish for the ocean's most powerful bounty in one of the most temperamental bodies of water. When you prefer to fish an area called No Man's Land, you can't risk anything. John's main concerns were safety and "getting that fucking fish in the boat."

John specializes in catching swordfish. Big swordfish. The kind of fish that haunt an angler's dreams. No other animal in the ocean has the ferocity, muscle and attitude of a broadbill swordfish. Anglers who dream of catching big swordfish, and I'm talking 600- to 800-pound beasts, usually end up on this boat, in this piece of ocean, fishing with this man.

"So here's the deal," John said. "As I told you, I'm giving you a reduced rate. We'll call this a split charter. There's one other angler on board, and we're charging him two-thirds the full rate. You, Mr. McPhee, are only going to be charged one-third."

"I don't get it," I said. "I mean I'm fine with it, but I just want to fish, John. What's the deal?"

"You make me laugh, Parker, and I'm going to need some comic relief on this one."

I had just traveled a total of 48 hours to sit on this boat on this dock in the Bay of Islands on New Zealand's far north coast. My flight from Los Angeles to Auckland took 13 hours. Then I got stuck in the airport in Auckland. Fog shut the whole place down. Instead of a one-hour flight north to Kerikeri, I ended up taking a six-hour bus ride. The countryside was pretty and all, but my ass turned into a pancake. I was constipated, dehydrated, jet-lagged and just plain hazy. I was ready for a stiff drink, a long nap and a good shit.

All of that travel, the expense and the headache would be well worth it if I got to reel in a big swordfish, but John's comment had me wondering what I'd signed up for.

"This doesn't sound good," I said.

John looked at me with a menacing smile. His icy blue eyes were hiding something. He ran a hand through his thick, silver, steel-wool hair and leaned in close, a crooked smile staring me down.

John was a serious guy, and not one to joke about much of anything. When guys like him smiled, it wasn't because something funny had just happened. Their thoughts were on the adventure ahead, the journey, the plan. Something was afoot.

I reeled back a bit as he held his head within three inches of my nose.

"You're not going to kiss me, are you, John?" I asked, trying to crack the ice.

"Nah, mate," John said in his thick New Zealand brogue, "but you just got fucked."

"I don't get it," I said.

"Hey, Marvin, come have a look at your fishing buddy!" John hollered.

I felt the boat heave just an inch or two as a walrus-size man waddled out of the salon. Surely this man couldn't be joining us on a nine-day run to fish the famed swordfish grounds near the rugged offshore islands known as the Three Kings. The large man looked around and spotted us sitting on the bridge.

"What da fuck a ya doin' up there?" he asked.

John kept staring at me, his blue eyes dancing, but responded to the man below. "C'mon up. I want you to meet Parker McPhee, your fishing buddy for the next nine days."

I shook my head.

The man slowly made his way up the bridge ladder, stopping at each rung to catch his breath and brace for the next step. When his big bald head came into view, I thought about jumping overboard.

I'd never seen a man with Marvin's skin tone. He was gray. His skin resembled that color you see in a boiled egg right where the white meets the yolk. It's not white or yellow — it's a strange drab gray. That's what this man's skin looked like. The gray innards of a boiled egg.

He finally descended onto the bridge deck, panting as if he'd just crested Everest. I peered down at him, speechless. Marvin looked like Darth Vader without his black mask.

"Hah ... hah ... hah ... ya doin?" he said, trying to suck some breath into his poor lungs. I felt sorry for his lungs.

"I'm okay," I said.

"Marvin, this here is Parker McPhee," John said. "He's the man I've been telling you about. Parker is an ace fisherman. Surprisingly good, really. We're going to need him on the boat when we're out there."

"Ah, gotcha," Marvin said. "So Parka, where ya from?"

I focused on the bald gray man in front of me. He was wearing a crew-neck sweatshirt, and white scraggly hairs stuck out of the neck hole like daddy longlegs. His skin was bumpy and rumpled. Large freckles dotted the top of his bald head. The few wiry hairs he had on the top of his noggin stuck up and hung over like wilted hay.

"Whatta ya deaf?" he said.

"I'm sorry, did you call me 'Parka'?" I asked.

"Well, it's yer name, ain't it?"

"So where in New York are you from, Marvin?" I asked.

"Jersey," he said. "Worked in Manhattan like all the other more-rons, but live in Jersey."

I nodded and looked back at John. "How many days are we going for?"

I stayed at a nearby hotel that night. After a bottle of wine and a venison tenderloin, I was completely wiped. I fell asleep early and didn't wake up for 12 hours. All of the travel and the horror of meeting Marvin had taken a major toll on me. But what was I going to do? I didn't fly halfway around the world to sit in a hotel. I had dreamt about fishing the famed Three Kings for most of my adult life. These are storied grounds.

John picked Marvin and me up the next morning. Marvin's color had improved some. This might not be so bad, I thought.

When we got to the boat, the mates were already there, busy storing the provisions for our nine-day trip. The plan was to motor 250 miles offshore, heading north into the Tasman Sea.

As we left the dock in the Bay of Islands, the seas were calm, leaving me with a grateful feeling. The weather acts like a temperamental supernova in these parts. Bombing low-pressure systems can descend on the fishing grounds. The barometer can drop 24 bars in the span of a day. Seas can climb from nothing to 18 feet in a matter of a few hours. The winds can go from a slight gust to 40 knots over the course of a morning — a scary thought since this boat will be our only shelter for the next nine days, with nothing but water underneath us.

John custom-built the boat, the *Broadbill*, for the sole purpose of fishing these turbulent seas. He chose to place the galley aft against the bulkhead for two reasons. First, the rear of a ship remains more stable when running in heavy seas. The bow will rise and pound more than the stern. The aft galley also keeps the deckhand who is preparing the food closer to the cockpit. If a fish raises up behind the boat and decides to snatch a lure, the mate can quickly get out of the galley and help out in the pit.

Forward of the galley sat a U-shaped dinette table with comfortable seating for six (or four if you were sitting with Marvin). A couch sat across from the table and converted to a berth. Stepping down to the forecabin revealed the sleeping quarters. Two double-bunk staterooms lined the starboard side while a larger stateroom to port offered a double berth and a small bunk. A large head with shower sat just in front of the port stateroom. There was also a day head right off the cockpit so you didn't need to track fish blood and salt water through the cabin to use the toilet. The master stateroom was situated all the way forward with a double bed and copious storage lining the walls and under the bunk. We packed the master with all of our gear. All of our sleeping would take place in the bunks, and the captain took only short naps away from the helm, usually on the couch in the salon.

The deck of the boat felt extremely large for a 58-footer. We needed to carry extra fuel to run for nine days. The crew filled up two collapsible fuel bladders, one with 740 liters of diesel and one with 500. The boys secured the big balls of fuel to the gunwales, or sides of the boat. A large icebox held drinks and fruit, while a custom-built workstation sat against the bulkhead.

"The workstation is strictly off-limits," John told Marvin. "Hooks, knives and pliers become dangerous instruments in rolling seas. No cameras, drinks or jackets are allowed on or around this workstation. This space belongs to the mates."

"Well, it really belongs to you, ain't that right, Captain?" Marvin asked.

"No. Like I said, this space belongs to the mates."

The flybridge offered U-shaped seating in front of the console and a single helm chair behind the dashboard with no companion chair. John needed room to swing his giant feet around as he moved from scanning his instrument panel to looking forward to monitoring the spread of lures behind the boat. His electronics were extremely high-tech for a charter operation. He had a commercial-grade sonar machine for spotting bait and game fish below the boat. His chartplotter featured the latest marine cartography available and his long list of treasured waypoints.

John kept a detailed log of everything he saw. He could show me the exact GPS coordinates of swordfish catches dating back eight years. With each mark, he noted the date, size of the fish, water temperature and angler name. If you want to be a top captain, you need to take notes like this.

The sun began to fade off as we continued our trek north. The

Southern Cross, the famous four-star constellation seen only in the Southern Hemisphere, came into view as the sky darkened. Weather conditions remained calm as we chugged along through these turbulent waters. We'd be fishing where the Tasman Sea runs smack into the South Pacific Ocean in a patch of water called Johnson's Trough, where currents boil and don't mix well with opposing winds.

Rounding North Point we saw Cape Reinga in the distance, the northernmost point of New Zealand, and kept on chugging.

In John's former life he ran commercial fishing vessels. That's how he learned to use depth sounders to their full capacity. Understanding the full power of a sounder and harnessing all of that machine's ability is a skill that takes years at sea to conquer. John installed the best transducer money could buy in the hull of his boat. This piece of equipment sends out signals into the water that bounce off the ocean floor and whatever other objects it encounters, pinging a signal back to the transducer. The sounder processes this information and displays the bottom contours on the screen, revealing any structure where the fish might be hiding, or even better, the actual fish. When you're riding along offshore for days on end, the depth sounder becomes a source of hope and entertainment. You find things. You become a treasure hunter. John is a master treasure hunter who has found just about every hump, lump and canyon edge along New Zealand's northern fishing grounds.

I tracked down a bottle of rum and made myself a few drinks, then I went up to the bridge to escape Marvin and dozed off on the settee. I don't know how long I was out, but I woke up when the captain pulled the throttles back.

"Time to fish," John said. It was a gorgeous night. Stars littered the night sky like a shotgun blast that peppered a street sign. The two mates danced around the deck like a pair of bats chasing down mosquitoes. Harry, the second mate, was 22, and Billy, the first mate, was nearing 30 and married. The boys loved to joke with each other, making cracks about Marvin when he was out of earshot — a dangerous move when your take-home pay depends on the tip the big man might leave you but a move I adored and happily engaged in. My plan was to hang out with Harry, Billy and John, and do my best to avoid Marvin at all costs.

The boys lined up their tools for night fishing — a monster 14/0 circle hook, fresh-caught squid, 600-pound leader material, rigging needles and waxed floss. I watched as Billy rigged up a single squid with a circle hook. He took his time, making each poke and knot of the floss precise. He sewed up the body of the squid with the floss, creating a small U-shaped piece of floss at the top of the squid. He looped the circle hook onto this piece of floss. The hook wasn't actually inserted into the body of the squid. Circle hooks get a better bite onto a fish's jaw when they're free from the bait, usually rigged to run in front of the bait.

John and his crew fished only a single swordfish bait at night, between 100 and 300 feet down depending on the amount of current. They attached a light strobe about 30 feet above the bait. This light could be seen for a long distance in the deep dark depths and will grab the attention of any nearby predators. The mates chose to fish just one bait because they didn't want to tangle with two of these giant swordfish simultaneously. That would almost certainly end in disaster.

Once the bait was deployed we began the waiting game. The boys cooked up some steaks and veggies while Marvin told stories of his fishing prowess.

"Parka, you ever been to Tropic Star?"

"No, Marvin," I said. "Never been."

"You call yourself a fisherman? Faaawk, I been down there to Panama every year since 1981," he said, wheezing in between syllables.

"That's nice, Marvin," I said.

"I caught four fah-king mah-lin in a single day down there. Four!" he yelled, spittle flying at me like mini asteroids.

"Impressive," I said, wiping my forehead with a napkin.

"You ever caught four fah-king blue mah-lin in a day, Parka?"

"Nope, can't say I have."

He laughed, his belly moving up and down like the pendulum on an oil rig.

"I didn't think so," he said.

Marvin was clearly enjoying himself out here on the boat, doing manly shit, chasing giant swordfish and busting balls. Everything about him repulsed me, except his willingness to travel to find the ocean's largest game fish. His accent gave me shivers. His relentless ribbing made me avoid conversations with him as much as possible, but old Marvin had to have some redeeming qualities, I thought to myself. He must have friends ... a wife?

"So what do you do for a living, Marvin?" I asked.

"I worked my ass off for 30 years, and then I sold out," he said. "Let's put it this way: I was never afraid to work. God didn't give me good looks or even all that much smarts. So I worked."

I nodded. "That's very admirable," I said. "What type of work?"

"When I was 19 I got a job as a maintenance man at an office building in Midtown. I fixed things like busted fixtures or leaky pipes. I unclogged toilets. I mopped. I did whatever they asked me to do. When I was about 22 I got into an argument with the owner of that building and I quit. Decided to go out on my own. I bought some supplies, got a truck and went out looking for work."

"How'd you find clients?" I asked.

"I knocked on fah-king doors, Parka. This ain't brain surgery. I was cheaper than the competition and worked twice as hard. Day and night, I was on call. Someone clogged the executive bathrooms in a midnight bender; I came in and took care of it. But the big difference came when I got in with the paper-goods people. I started selling all the paper supplies to my accounts. I sold enough fah-king toilet paper to wipe the entire world's ass. I hired crews to take care of the maintenance and janitorial services, and I sold the paper goods. Every time some suit took a shit in Midtown, that was money in my fah-king bank account," he said, laughing, his belly bouncing like that little ball jumping from word to word in a kid's tune.

"You're like the toilet paper king of New York," I said. "Who knew? Interesting story, Marvin. I'm going to step outside and see what the boys are up to."

I slid the salon door open and the salty breeze moistened my skin. I closed my eyes, breathed deeply, taking in the ocean's sweet perfume.

The wind had begun to pick up a bit, but it wasn't blowing steady, it was just enough to toss my hair around a little. I took inventory of the cockpit as best I could in the dark. John had two massive lights set on the hardtop above the flybridge, but these remained off while fishing. He'd switch them on when a rod came tight to a swordfish, lighting up the cockpit like Yankee Stadium. Right now, the battlefield lay under the cover of darkness. As my eyes adjusted to the lack of light, I could make out objects around the deck. Marvin's shoulder harness hung from the fighting chair. I picked up the harness, a canvas vest with two strands of rope that clipped the harness to the lugs on the top of the fishing reel with stainless-steel carabiners. This piece of padded fabric locks the angler to the reel. Once attached to the rod and reel with the harness, an angler can use his or her entire body to fight a fish. The harness keeps you attached to the rod and reel so you don't have to hold onto the rod with your hands and use your shoulders and biceps to lift the rod. The hands remain on the reel at all times, and the angler can let his ass come off the chair by pinning his feet to the footrest. Once in this position, the trick is to throw your head back, using the weight of your entire body to put pressure on a big fish. This lifts or loads the rod so the angler can crank in line as the rod tip falls back down toward the surface of the ocean.

Personally, when fishing from a fighting chair, I prefer a bucket harness that is more like a little seat for your ass. This type of harness suits my build. I'm lean and get more strength out of my lower body. Marvin is built like a beer keg. He puts on the shoulder harness, locks it to the reel and uses that pendulum to swing the rod back so it loads up against the fish. With big fish, every inch counts. Pump and grind, pump and grind.

I sat down on the mezzanine and stared out at the horizon. The minutes faded away, the sound of the diesel engines hummed along and my thoughts began fading off to other lands. Marvin must've fallen asleep. The boys were either in their bunks or relieving the captain on the bridge. Quiet. I put my head down and closed my eyes.

"Fish on!" John yelled down from the helm, breaking the

silence in his thick New Zealand brogue. "FISH ON!"

I opened my eyes and couldn't see a thing. The captain had switched on the lights, illuminating the cockpit and water behind the boat like a freaking parking lot. My pupils were blinded.

"Parker, go wake up Marvin. Lads, get on deck!" John said loudly.

I opened the door to the salon and found Marvin staggering toward the cockpit in his underwear, struggling to pull up his pants while keeping his momentum. I cowered away from him, closing my eyes. The scraggly daddy longlegs were all over him!

I tried to yell, 'Get your ass on deck, Marvin, we've got a fucking swordfish on' but managed only a slight 'fish on' as I looked away.

Marvin moved faster than I could've predicted and hopped into the fighting chair, chest harness on and ready to battle. "I'm ready!" he yelled. "Gimme the fah-king rod, Billy! What the fahk?"

"Sorry, Marvin, he's off," Billy said. "I don't think he was ever hooked. Sometimes these broadbills just take a swipe to kill their prey even if they're not that interested in eating it. I think it just pulled some line but never came tight."

"You're fah-king kiddin' me right now. Was this some sort of test? You wanted to see how fast you could make me move, didn't you, you little shit?"

We couldn't tell if Marvin was joking around. The boys shrugged their shoulders and looked up at John on the bridge.

"We had a nice fish on, Marvin," John said. "I made the call and I don't appreciate you talking to my crew like that."

"Your crew, eh? Oh, I see how it is, Cappy," Marvin said. "You the one who tips 'em too, eh? Fuck this. I can get to this chair faster than any of yews. So just get the fahk outta my way when you really hook one, okay? Don't forget, I caught four fah-king mah-lins in one day down in Panama. One fah-king day!"

Billy unclipped Marvin's harness and pulled the big rod out of the gimbal in the fighting chair.

"Some of them just come off, man," I said. "It's nobody's fault."

The old man scowled at me and muttered something under his breath as he tossed his harness onto the mate's table, the one spot

John had asked Marvin not to mess with.

"I'll be ready for the next one," he said and went back into the cabin.

The boys reeled in the bait and saw a six-inch-long slash on the 10-pound lead weight they used to keep the squid down deep in the bite zone. Billy lifted the weight up and showed it to John on the bridge.

"Bloody hell," John said. "You have any idea how hard you have to hit a piece of lead underwater to make a slash like that? He's here, gents. Our fish is here."

Out of the corner of my eye I saw Marvin's bulbous figure moving about in the cabin. He dropped trou, leaving his pants on the floor and laid down on the sofa. I went up to the bridge. John was writing in his logbook, noting the time of night, the state of the tide, location and water temperature. "We're in the zone, Parker," he said. "You're up next. Be ready."

"I'm always ready," I said, smiling.

The stadium lights came back on around two a.m. The rod keeled over, taking on the shape of a taco. Line flew off the reel. The clicker on the reel sounded like an angry Harley-Davidson. I leapt down off the bridge onto the deck, pulled the rod out of the holder, side-stepped to the fighting chair and made my way onto the seat, settling into the bucket harness that Billy had left in the perfect position for me to jump right into. I grabbed the ropes on each side of the harness, attached them to the reel and put my hands over the spool, trying to keep the line from bouncing as it poured off. This fish was not 'fah-king' around.

"Turn that bloody clicker off!" John yelled. I obliged. "Increase the drag to 15 kilos." I slowly moved the lever drag up to the 15 mark one of the mates had made with a magic marker on a blue piece of electrical tape that ran up the side of the reel.

"It's a big fish, Parker, but I'm not sure it's the one we're after. Let's gain some line on the bugger," Billy said.

The captain swung the boat around as Billy spun the fighting chair to keep me in line with the direction the fish was heading. As the boat came about, I was able to retrieve several cranks of line. Fighting a big swordfish requires expert boat handling, which takes a little more care when the only illumination you have are a few million stars and a set of stadium lights. Many captains have driven right over the fishing line in the heat of battle. Adrenaline tends to get the best of a fisherman, whether he's got a fishing rod in his hands or a steering wheel.

I used my left hand to lay the fishing line evenly on the reel as I cranked and cranked with my right hand to keep tension on the line. John bumped the boat in and out of gear.

"Doing great, Parker," he said. "I see the swivel." The barrel swivel marks the point where the running line is connected to the leader, the much heavier, final trace of line. The boys had an 800-pound-test leader on this rig to keep us tight to the mighty sword.

The bill on a swordfish is flat like a paddle and covered in tiny bumps. Even if the fish is hooked in the mouth, the abrasive bill can slowly tear its way through the leader as the fish swings its head back and forth trying to free itself. The thick 600-pound monofilament nylon will hold for a long time on most fish. If the hooked animal is a shark, odds are you'll get cut off, unless the shark is hooked right in the corner of the mouth so the metal hook is the only thing that the animal's teeth come in contact with.

"Harry, you got your gloves on?" John asked. Harry stuck his hands in the air, showing that he was already wearing the thick wiring gloves. The mate's most important piece of equipment are his gloves. They are the only protection he has when he grabs the leader to pull the giant animal the last 20 or 30 feet to the boat. Harry made his own gloves, using a pair of mechanic's gloves stuck inside heavy-duty welding gloves. In between the two pairs, he sewed some padding on for an extra layer of protection. When you take a proper wrap of the line, the pressure is on the top of the hand. If you're unseasoned and don't know when to let go, you can easily crush a hand on a big swordfish. Harry said every pair of gloves he ever bought fell apart after a few fish, but his homemade gloves lasted two or more seasons.

Each man on a game boat has a role. The captain finds the fish and maneuvers the boat to help the angler catch the target animal. The captain is also responsible for maintaining all systems and the safety of the crew. He's the CEO of the vessel. The mates take care of the tackle, checking every knot, every hook, every inch of line. These boys rig bait after bait and are the keepers of the boat. The operational managers, if you will. They wash, they dry, they change oil, they make food, they work nonstop. The reason they do all of this manual labor is for the end game: the chance to grab the leader and yank on a giant fish. There's no reel or hardware involved in the end game, just brawn and brains. You have to know how to wrap your hands in the leader and more importantly, when to let go, so you don't break that mono or get yanked into the inky dark water. Harry, our younger mate, lived for this moment, while Billy, the more experienced, watched his every step, keeping close by should something go wrong. If the leader got wrapped around the rod tip or Harry's hands got locked up, Billy would spring into action. He always had a small knife on him just in case he had to cut a fish off to save a man.

I could see the swivel getting close. Harry leaned out over the covering board, getting ready to grab the line. I'd gain an inch, lose an inch. The fish was stalling out under the boat.

"Put the heat to it, Parker," said John. I bumped the drag up a bit more, and Harry grabbed the line and pulled it toward his waist.

Harry looked back at me in the fighting chair: "Sorry, mate," he said. "This one's not the sword you're looking for. It's a mako shark."

Harry looked up at the captain, and I could hear John mumble a few curses just as the fish came up to the surface.

At some point Marvin had made his way onto the deck and started talking in my ear. "Can't catch no sword, eh Parka?"

"Not now, Marvin," I said.

"Ever eaten mako, Parka? Tastes like sword, but it's not!" His belly bounced like a beach ball as he roared in laughter.

The boys got a tag stick ready so they could tag the fish before we released it. The small nylon tags help scientists study the movements and growth patterns of fish. Each tag carries a number

SUCKED DRY

on it and the name of the tagging agency. The crew puts the tag in the fish's back where the small piece of nylon won't interfere with anything, and then they release the fish. The crew also fills out a card with information about the fish they just tagged, noting the tag number, date, location, species and size of the fish when it was caught. If that fish is recovered, the tag is retrieved and the size and location is again noted. This way researchers can determine how far the fish swam while at large and how much it grew.

The boys pulled the shark next to the boat, and Harry warned us that the fish was going to go nuts after they tagged it. Sure as shit, just when Billy stuck the fish with the tag, the mako swiped its tail, sending a wall of water right into Marvin's face. What a good little shark.

The next morning I awoke to an eerie quiet. After three days of constant motoring, the engines were off. No droning drum of pistons pushing. No exhaust swooping out the back of the boat. All quiet on deck.

I peeked out the small porthole in my bunk and spotted the craggy, gray moon rock of one of the islands that make up the Three Kings. I couldn't determine if the rock looked welcoming or menacing. The Three Kings lie some 38 miles off the tip of Cape Reinga. The explorer Abel Tasman stumbled upon these landforms in the mid-1600s. He found them during the Christmas holiday and decided to name them the Three Kings, though there are actually 13 islands. We anchored right in the lee of Great Island, the largest. All was quiet. Strangely quiet.

I crawled out of my bunk and found Billy cooking breakfast in the galley.

"This must be the Three Kings," I said. "I've read about this place."

"Sure is, mate," Billy said. "What do you think?"

"Kind of creepy."

Billy laughed: "I can tell you this: These islands have saved our ass many times. When you're all alone out here and it's blowing 50-plus, you start to thank God for these islands. Safe anchorage isn't easy to come by out here."

I nodded my head. "Does anyone live out here?"

97

"Nah, I believe there was a Maori colony out here back in the 1800s or something, but it's a pretty inhospitable place, to say the least," Billy said, stirring some hollandaise for the eggs benedict Marvin had requested.

"These islands play an important role in Maori religion," Billy said, referring to New Zealand's indigenous people. "There is a rare tree that only lives here called the Kaikomako. According to legend, the dead spirits seek out these islands so they can crawl down the roots and return to the sea, or something like that."

I stepped onto the deck of the boat, looking straight up at the rocky landscape. I didn't see a single tree or much flora of any kind. It made me wonder how the hell anyone could survive out here. The only other life around us were colonies of royal albatross, a giant seabird with a wingspan of 10 feet. I watched two birds circling high above the rocky island, riding an upwelling like a jet-shaped puff of cotton. It made me think of "The Rime of the Ancient Mariner," an epic poem that I had read in college or high school, I forget which. I wondered if this crew would go mutinous and rebel against the captain for allowing the big man onto the vessel. Surely we'd die trying to hang him around our necks.

Guys like Marvin don't hold the sea's creatures in much regard. To him, catching a fish is all about bravado. A fish is nothing more than something you mount and put on the office wall so you can point to it every time a visitor walks in and boast about an expensive trip to Alaska or Central America. It's a way to show off. There is some joy in the journey, no doubt, but much more joy in the trophy. The journey is only a necessity for Marvin to get his hands on the trophy. I fish for the opposite reason. I fish for the adventure. For the sense of not knowing what I may encounter every time we round the last buoy on our way out of some newfound harbor and hit the throttles. That's the romance of it, for me. It's the unknown that keeps me up all night with anticipation. It's the people you meet. The places you find yourself in. I don't need any more mounts on my wall. I guess I am my father's son in that way. Daddy caught his share of trophy fish and traveled to the world's best fishing spots, but he would never throw it in someone's face. He'd never open a conversation by asking if someone had been to the most expensive fishing lodge on earth just so he could brag that he had. That was not why he fished. He fished because he fucking loved to do it.

From the Three Kings, John had put us within easy access of King Bank and Middlesex Bank. Depending on the weather and current, he planned to target several of his most productive marlin spots. He studied his numbers, planning our hunt of striped marlin during the day and our targeted species, the broadbill swordfish, at night.

After breakfast, John fired up the diesel engines and the boys pulled up the anchor. We headed back out on the great search for billfish.

I spent time on the flybridge asking John why the striped marlin grow so large in New Zealand. In most other places in the world, such as Mexico's Baja Peninsula, the striped marlin are ankle biters compared to those found off the North Island. In Mexico, a 180-pound striped marlin would be considered a beast. In New Zealand, they don't start getting excited until that fish hits the 300-pound mark. John said it's the abundance of bait in these colder waters that help the stripeys grow so large, and I wasn't about to disagree with him.

I spotted large schools of sauries skipping across the swells like innocent school kids as we motored on. The saury is a long, slender silvery baitfish that looks a tad like a ballyhoo without the beak. We cruised for about an hour before John eased the throttles and lifted his large frame off the helm chair so he could reach back and set down the outriggers. Harry and Billy began to set out a spread of four teasers and four hooked lures. We ran two teasers off the bridge lines. John himself would man these teasers which were really just large lures without any hooks. One was a blunt-faced custom lure about the size of an eight-year-old's leg. It had a purple-and-black skirt over a silver skirt attached to the lure head and concealing much of the hook-set. The big lure pushed an impressive amount of water and left a long trail of bubbles and white water behind it as the boat pulled it along. The other bridge teaser consisted of a daisy chain of plastic squid. There were eight squid total, each one with wide wings that flapped across the surface of the water, creating a splashing effect that will grab the attention of a billfish in any ocean. Not many New Zealanders use the squid chain, but John saw it work in the Caribbean during his travels and always ran one.

The boys in the cockpit manned the other teasers. Off one corner of the transom, they employed a Witch Doctor, a crazy-looking teaser that was originally created from a table leg. It had mirrors all over it and colorful streaks of green and yellow. On the other corner, they kept it simple, running a large bonito belly behind a green plunger-style lure with a cupped face designed to push water on the surface. The four hook baits were all run out of the outriggers so the boys could place the baits wide and away from the white wash behind the boat. The lure pattern was spread out and staggered, which is why anglers call it a "spread."

The mates worked quickly and efficiently setting out the lures, making sure each jig swam as it should. As the boys moved from rod to rod, John watched for any signs of life — birds, whales, busting bait or free-jumping billfish.

Marvin stayed in the cabin of the boat, trying to figure out how to get a movie to play on the boat's DVD player. He'd already watched all of the movies on board, but he wasn't one for reading or thinking, really. He had brought *The Perfect Storm* with him. Can you fucking believe that? Traveling 200 miles offshore and this idiot plops *The Perfect Storm* into DVD player. There's nothing more fun than watching a crew go down with the ship as you're sitting on a chunk of fiberglass in the middle of the ocean.

As a deckhand, you're trained to keep your eyes on the spread of baits or lures behind the boat at all times. If you see any disturbance such as a big shadow trailing a lure, a flash of color or the swat of a marlin's bill, you yell out the location of whatever it is you saw, hoping it's a billfish: "Left short!" The yell kicks the rest of the crew into gear. Just because you're trolling a spread of lures doesn't mean you can get lax and wait for the reel's clicker to go off, especially with four teasers behind the boat. The teaser does exactly what its name implies: It teases a fish into the spread of lures behind the boat. The mates may then draw the fish closer and closer to the transom by reeling in the teaser as the fish repeatedly whacks the fish-mimicking piece of plastic or natural bait. Few things infuriate a big marlin more than pulling food out of its mouth.

After the crew draws the enraged fish to the boat, the angler drops his or her bait into the water and places it next to the teaser. With the hook bait in position, the crewman yanks the teaser out of the water. What happens next is called the bait-and-switch. The enraged marlin will turn and pounce on the hook bait like a starved bear trying to swipe a candy bar out of some fat tourist's hand.

The term "bait-and-switch" has been used by just about every industry throughout the world, and it works pretty much the same way no matter what the teaser happens to be — wealth, gorgeous women, drugs — they all work well on men. For marlin, it's usually a big lure or a dead bait pulled behind the boat. The result, no matter the bait, is pretty much the same when performed properly, although not everyone chasing down a line of coke or the salty inner thigh of a blond Peruvian will practice catch-and-release. That's a different story entirely.

We hadn't seen another boat all morning. We were all alone, just the way John liked it, as we motored at seven knots across the 1,000-fathom edge under clear skies and a on somewhat calm sea, well, calm by Kiwi standards. The winds were a light and variable 18 knots, kicking up a four-foot chop with short-period waves that the boat easily cut through. A random six-footer kicked up a tad of spray. Ideal conditions for this type of fishing.

"Right long! Right long!" John's voice rang down from the bridge, breaking up the ongoing drone of the diesel engines that had hardly gotten a break since we departed days earlier.

The crew bounced into action and I was first to the rod. Marvin was 30 minutes into *Freaky Friday*, a mother-daughter switcheroo flick starring Jamie Lee Curtis, one of Marvin's favorite actresses.

The line on the right long rigger was yanked out of the outrigger clip when the fish struck the bait, but I wasn't hooked up. I pulled the rod out of the holder and hoisted the rod tip up as high as I could, trying to bring the lure back up to the surface so

John could get a better glimpse of it from the flybridge.

"It's clean," he said. "He buggered off."

I reeled in some of the line and motioned the rod tip to Billy so he could grab the line and set it back into the outrigger.

John began a wide turn back toward the area where we got bit. Turning is a strange thing when pulling lures. As you turn the boat, the change in direction slows the troll for a few minor moments and the lures tend to work their way down a few inches or sometimes even a foot or more if you turn sharply. This change in depth can trigger a bite. And sure as shit, as the boat worked its way starboard, the two longs went down, cracking out of the outrigger halyards simultaneously. Unlike the first bite, both of these marlin were not coming off. Billy let out a high-pitched, girlish-sounding scream as he grabbed the right long and engaged the drag to make sure the hook was set. I grabbed the left and did the same, scanning the waves behind the boat to see if my fish would leap into the air.

"Marvin, get out here!" Billy yelled. "We've got a double on, mate."

There was no movement in the cabin.

"Marvin!" John hollered, pounding on the floor of the flybridge with his sasquatch-size foot to command the fat man out of the cabin. Harry went inside in search of Marvin while both Billy and I lost line to two big fish we'd yet to see.

Line poured off the reels, the two fish bolting in opposite directions. I looked up to the captain and held out my reel so he could see my spool and monitor how much line was left on the reel. I didn't have to say anything. With more than half of the line gone, it was time to make a call. We'd have to chase down these fish, one at a time. Fat man or no fat man.

"Billy, hang on, we're going after Parker's fish first," John said.

The captain spun the boat expertly, throwing one engine in forward and the other in reverse and bumping up the RPMs to work our way toward my fish, bow first. The growing chop made a long back-down in reverse a very wet and potentially dangerous endeavor. Billy stood on the gunwale and held his rod high with one hand while he clenched the grab rail with his other. With the rod tip high, Billy kept his line out of the way as I cranked and cranked as fast as I could on the lever-drag reel to gain back as much of the 80-pound running line as I could.

"Doing good, Parker," John said in a relaxed tone. "Not much longer now. Billy, you okay?"

"All good but getting pretty low on line, Cappy," Billy said.

The difference between a good crew and a novice one is the way they handle these high-anxiety moments. Screaming, swearing, swinging gaffs and tossing around gear is for amateurs who can't control their adrenaline. No yelling, calm movements and a rushed but safe rate of operation are the hallmarks of a good crew

I could see the knot from the double line make its way out of the ocean, which meant I was getting close to the fish. It was coming in nice and easy, or so I thought. John kicked the ass end of the boat around as the boys got ready for the end game.

Harry came out of the cabin, putting on his wiring gloves. He looked up to the captain and informed us that Marvin had fallen asleep.

"Fuck it," John said. "Get ready to wire this fish, Harry, and we'll go after the other one."

Harry placed both hands on the transom of the boat and bent down into a half-squat like a Sumo wrestler. Billy held his rod high to keep the back of the boat clear from any tangles, but he didn't have much line left on the reel. The lack of line didn't seem to worry him, though.

I pushed the drag up just a tad to help me winch in the last few feet of line needed to pull the double line out of the waves and through the rod tip. Once that knot breaches the guide at the tip of the rod, that, for many anglers, signifies a catch. But I still hadn't seen the ... oh wait, there she is! The eight-foot-long, silvery-blue billfish leapt straight out of the water 10 feet off the transom, like a missile shot out of a submarine, heading straight for the heavens. The fish was flanked in bands of an electric blue that was so vivid it was nearly purple. Its pectoral fins glowed with a deep neon sapphire punctuated by a splattering of dark spots.

The power of the animal yanked me to the side of the boat.

Harry had helped me strap into a fighting belt and harness at the start of the fight so I could battle the fish standing up instead of using the fighting chair. That was my choice and I regretted it for a second.

"Hundred kilos," John said. "Easily. Maybe a few more."

That's 220 pounds. No slouch for a striped marlin, and my biggest by far. The fish was a good hundred yards off the transom when the captain began laying on the throttles to gain back the line. A black puff of exhaust smoke billowed out of the boat as the turbos spooled up and the boat jumped backward closing the gap between me and the fish in a few heartbeats. Harry reached out to grab the leader. Once the young deckhand had the line in his gloved hand, he got down into a half-squat to keep his center of gravity low and took a wrap of line around his hand. Then another. He'd swing his right hand clockwise and his left hand counter-clockwise to wrap the line around his hands so he could pull the fish closer. In a mere seconds the tired fish was beside the boat.

"Grab the tag stick, Parker," the captain said. "It's ready to go."

I eased the drag some, unclipped my belt and put my rod in the holder so I could grab the tag stick.

For many years, John tagged the most striped marlin in the world each and every season. But it's a numbers game. Only a handful of his fish were ever recaptured. One was caught two years later just a few miles from its original spot. Another one swam 1,200 miles in just nine months. That's what makes studying these fish so difficult. You need a lot of data to formulate a hypothesis, and getting the data is not easy.

Harry grabbed the bill of the fish and worked the hook free. The fish was now unattached and held only by the young man's hand.

"Go for it," Harry said.

I reached over and placed the tag halfway down the silvery dark back of the striped marlin, just below the fish's dorsal. The tag sparked whatever fight the fish had left in it, and the neon animal disappeared in a flash. Harry looked at me with a huge smile and smacked me on my back.

"Nice work, Parker. You ready for round two?"

I almost forgot we still had another fish hooked. John pounded on the flybridge floor and screamed for Marvin yet again. Harry went into the cabin and shook Marvin awake for a second. In between snores and a coughing fit, Marvin asked if the fish was a sword. When Harry told him it was a striped marlin, he cursed out the young mate for waking him and went back to sleep. Harry stood up and thought about choking out Marvin for a second but did the sane thing and walked away. He heard Marvin mutter something about keeping his stamina for the evening bite. I, for one, was grateful that he didn't want to catch what could potentially be a 300-pound striped marlin.

Billy handed me the rod with striped marlin number two, which had pulled damn near all of the line off the reel. The shiny spool winked at me in between the hi-vis green fishing line remaining on the reel.

"Oh shit," I said. "I can see the fucking knot. How much line does this reel hold?"

"Twelve-hundred yards."

I dropped my head but couldn't contain my smile.

"You want to get in the fighting chair?" Billy asked.

"Nah, I already got the belt on."

We trolled until the sun dipped into the ocean on the western horizon. We caught one more striped marlin on the day, and saw a few more. Marvin never left the confines of the cabin. At one point, I stuck my head into the salon and found him passed out on the couch with his hand in a bag of purple and red gummy bears. It was my favorite afternoon on the boat since leaving the dock. Just me and the crew and a massive ocean to play in.

As the sky darkened, Billy relieved John on the bridge. The captain hardly left the helm. He'd come down to the galley every few hours to brew himself a batch of instant coffee or some tea and maybe reload his pack of cigarettes. Caffeine and nicotine fuel most every fishing operation on the high seas.

John is about five inches short of what I'd call a giant. He's a solid six-foot-five with hands the size of baseball gloves and feet like surfboards. He has to duck to get through every doorway on the boat, which he does effortlessly and pretty much habitually.

This is one area he knows by heart and feel. I never saw him bang his head once, which people much shorter can't say when they're on board a vessel. He's not just tall — he's thick with a barrel chest and large, powerful shoulders and arms. His face is surprisingly friendly and augmented with bright-blue eyes and thick, black hair, which always looks perfect. He wears a cap all day to help him see the horizon from the bridge and block out the bright sunlight, but when he takes off the hat after sitting atop his head for 12 hours, there is no discernable difference in his hair. His part is perfect. Wind can blow a solid 25 knots and his hair won't move; it'll just wave a bit at the tips, looking perfect. My hair usually looks like shit, even in favorable conditions.

John opened the oven to take a peek at dinner, and the aroma quickly filled the cabin.

"Pot roast and potatoes," he said. "We eat well tonight."

"We've been eating well every night," I said. "Your boys do a great job, John."

"Thanks, mate. They work their asses off. In case you didn't notice, I'm not an easy guy to work for," he said, starting to laugh. "You better eat fast so you can beat Marvin to the serving dish for seconds. And you'll need your strength. I have a feeling tonight's the night we get what we came all this way for."

I smiled, hoping his premonition had some truth to it, and that it wasn't some attempt to boost my spirits. We hadn't caught a sword yet and the trip was already half over.

Billy put the boat on autopilot at a very slow clip, heading into the four-foot swell at a slight beam-to angle. Marvin came to just in time for dinner (go figure), and for about an hour, we all sat around the dinette table, eating tender pot roast, quartered potatoes and steamed carrots. The boys opened a bottle of New Zealand pinot noir that Marvin and I drank. The boys abstained. For a bunch of smelly fishermen, we felt pretty fucking civilized.

After dinner we fell into our rehearsed routine. The boys cleaned off the plates. I offered to help with the dishes, but they wouldn't let me. John returned to his post on the bridge with a fresh cup of coffee and a new pack of cigarettes. Marvin moved to the couch, inserted a movie into the DVD player and proceeded to belch and pick his teeth with whatever was handy. He'd fold the corner of a magazine into a toothpick, use the point of a knife or even the hook from a trolling lure. The picking of the teeth didn't bother me nearly as much as the noise that preceded it as he desperately tried to suck out whatever debris was left in between his teeth with his tongue. It made a high-pitched sound like a stuck baby pig. I'd retreat to the cockpit or bridge at the first squeal.

Once the boys were done cleaning up from dinner, they moved out onto the deck and began setting out the swordfish gear. The big rod was armed with a Penn 130 International reel, its golden anodized coating shining brightly, even in the dim light. This is the largest recreational fishing reel you can buy. A few different companies make them, but not many fishermen have a lot of use for them. These reels are designed to battle the world's largest game fish. They call it heavy tackle for a reason. Made out of solid aluminum, the reels weigh more than a 10-pound dumbbell with an internal drag system that can impart 60 or more pounds of resistance against a big brute of an animal trying to swim in the opposite direction.

The rod took its position in the rod holder on the starboard side's covering board. The boys tinkered with the squid bait to get the circle hook situated perfectly. It went over the side into the pitch-black waters. After the leader was out, they connected the line to a downrigger ball and it set the bait down 100 feet. John put one engine in neutral and bumped the other in and out of gear to keep the bow into the current. You could call it a slow troll, but it didn't feel like the boat was moving at all, except rolling a bit with the slight swell. Now, we wait.

The night sky offshore is nothing short of spectacular. And when you're the lone boat out there, the stars become a singular source of entertainment. I found myself gazing up for hours. I'd find moving dots that I figured were satellites and did my best to discern the planets from the stars. The celestial beauty helped the time tick by in between bites.

You begin to tune out the drone of the diesel engines. Your mind escapes to all sorts of places. I thought of my nights out fishing with Daddy, staring at the skies of a different hemisphere. I could hear him in my head. "You know, Parker, the best part of being out on the boat at night is the sound of the waves slapping the hull." I love that sound.

I found myself empathizing with the fish we were after. Not that I wanted any of the swordfish to get away or come unhooked, but there were many times in my past where I narrowly escaped some sort of trouble or pain. I knew what it was like to be chased, enticed and hooked. I was lucky to escape. Any fish we came in contact with would not be so lucky.

Occasionally, I would take a nip from a rum bottle or doze off. I preferred being out in the fresh air as opposed to sitting next to Marvin or listening to his snores reverberate off the fiberglass walls of my bunk.

The sudden flare of the stadium lights pulled me out of my dreamscape like a doctor plucking a baby from its mother's womb. I sat up, blinked a few hundred times to clear the salty muck from my eyes, and noticed Billy and Harry moving quickly on a deck that was pitching much more than when I dozed off. I had no idea how long I'd been down. I slid off the mezzanine box I was resting on and was nearly bashed in the head by the salon door that flew open faster than one of Marvin's escaping farts. The big man waddled past in blazing speed, pulling on his foul-weather bibs with one hand and readying his chest harness with the other.

"Reel in the slack!" John yelled. "We got bit two minutes ago. Where the fuck were you, Marvin?"

"I'm here, I'm here," Marvin said, getting to the rod and cranking the big reel as fast as his sausage fingers could muster. The slack tightened and the rod took on the shape of a nice bow as it flexed against the power of the fish. Marvin pulled the rod from the rod holder and held it against his belly as he sidestepped over the foot pedestal and hoisted his big butt into the fighting chair. The boys did their best to help Marvin without touching the fishing line or rod in any way. Angling rules dictate that only the angler touches the rod, reel and line during a fish fight. Should anyone else aid the angler, the catch wouldn't be considered for world-record status.

"Knock 'em dead, big guy," I said and took ahold of the bridge ladder to keep myself steady on my feet. A dark wave slapped the stern of the boat and threw water onto Marvin's face, igniting a battle cry from the fat man that actually made me proud. His mouth opened huge like the jaws of a reticulated python. Marvin looked cartoonish in the fighting chair with his head kicked back and his mouth wide open yelling vulgarities, like a sock puppet or Homer Simpson.

Catching a big fish quickly and safely requires a full team: the captain, the angler, the deckhand, the leaderman who pulls in the last 10 yards of the heavy line by hand, a gaff man and a dude to move the fighting chair to keep a straight angle between man and fish. I was the chair driver. It took some might to move the chair with Marvin sitting in it, but I did my best to give him a clear, straight line on the fish. But these fish move quickly, and seeing the 100-pound-test line in the pitch-black night was challenging, even with the stadium lights illuminating 15 feet of water behind the vessel. The big guy cranked and cranked, gaining quickly, perhaps too quickly. I looked up to John, trying to gauge the look on his face to see if this fish might not be our targeted species. John looked down at me and shrugged his shoulders.

"I see color," Harry said. "I think it's a shark, maybe 200 kilos."

"Nah," Marvin said, balls of perspiration forming on his Vader-like bald head. "It's a swordfish, a fah-king swordfish, I can feel it!"

Harry shook his head. Marvin gained more line as John eased the boat into position for the boys to grab the leader. Harry reached out and pulled on the leader to bring the fish closer to the side of the boat where we could get a good look at it.

"Mako," John said. "Decent one. Put a tag in it and cut it loose."

"Fuck that, Cappy," Marvin said. "Gaff the thing. I want to hang it on my wall."

"Marvin, it's not worth it," John responded. "It'll cost you more to have it mounted and shipped back to the States than it would to go catch a mako off New York somewhere. It's not a trophy, mate. Let it go."

"Fuck this shit!" Marvin yelled, unclicking his harness from the lugs on the top of the fishing reel. He kicked the big rod out of the gimbal. Luckily Billy caught the rod and reel before it crashed onto the deck of the boat, potentially putting a big gash in John's treasured vessel. "I came here to catch a goddamn swordfish, not sharks, not kingfish, not tuna. You catch me a fucking swordfish!" Marvin's face reddened, and spittle flew as he yelled at the mighty captain.

No man had ever spoken to the captain like that, let alone from the deck of the man's own vessel. I think I may have closed my eyes for a couple of seconds, fearing bloodshed. I wanted to hold someone's hand, picturing John unleashing a weapon from his ditch bag and blasting Marvin between the eyes. Me and the mates were wide-eyed. Motionless.

John laughed: "Go inside, Marvin," he said, "before something very regrettable happens."

Marvin stared the captain down for a second or two, panting like a forlorn elephant before clearer heads prevailed. The fat man did the right thing and retreated into the cabin of the boat, slamming the door behind him.

"You're up, Parker," John said. "Let's get a bait back in the water, boys."

It didn't take long for Billy and Harry to change out the leader and pin on a fresh squid bait. They put out a good 25 feet of leader, maybe more, before they clipped the line to the heavy downrigger ball that would bring the squid and blinking strobe into the aphotic depths to attract our quarry. I watched the glimmer of the light sink down and finally disappear into the depths.

"Do your thing," I said to the bait, waving goodbye.

When the squid bait was at the correct depth and swaying its tentacles in the current, the captain switched off the stadium lights. Everything went completely black until my eyes adjusted to the evening.

The wind had come up since Marvin's shark. It was blowing out of the east. You didn't feel much when the captain ran with the wind, but every now and again a large swell would push the bow of the boat a few degrees over, giving the wind a more direct path to my face. The gusts felt colder on my cheeks and nose as the time inched past, and quite a bit stronger. The bow was pitching much more as the swells began to bunch closer together. Whitecaps formed on the crests of the larger waves. The safety lines hanging from the side of the boat swayed back and forth in a rhythmic dance. I used my core muscles to keep myself from sliding off my spot on the mezzanine.

Harry stopped the downrigger, tightening the drag down. Our bait was 250 feet below the surface. The mate took his hand off the downrigger and started to look up at John when the short barrel of the downrigger violently swept in toward the transom. The fishing line ripped from the clip below the surface and the big rod bent over in a loud thud, followed by the frantic buzzing of the reel's clicker.

"We're bit!" I yelled, leaping from the mezzanine. "We're fucking bit!"

The lights flipped on and the engines spooled up as the captain swung the bow around. I got to the reel, eased back on the drag just a hair so I could free the broomstick-thick rod from the holder, and walk it to the fighting chair. My heart was thumping like Keith Moon's bass drum and I tried to take a deep breath to calm my shaking hands. The blood was racing through me. My cheeks went flush. My legs became wobbly. I didn't want to slip on the deck.

"Easy, Parker," Billy said in a very calm voice. "Just step over the footrest and get into the chair. Nice and easy, mate. You've got this."

I stepped over the gimbal, rod against my hip, and managed to slide my ass onto the seat. I hadn't even noticed but the boys had already adjusted the chair after Marvin's shark, and the footrest was perfectly set for my five-foot, ten-inch frame. I placed the rod into the gimbal and got my second foot onto the footrest. Billy was behind me now and held out the clips for the bucket harness, which I had wedged under my ass cheeks. He held the harness clips next to my hands so I could easily take them and attach them to the lugs on the top of the reel. I was locked in. Tight to a giant animal lurking somewhere deep below the surface. The excitement erupted inside of me like a bomb, and a deep yell burst out of my mouth. AAAERRGAGGHEHHHH!

"Take it easy, Parker!" John scolded me from the bridge. "Ease the drag up mate, you need to stay tight to this fish."

I pushed the drag up to the strike button, but the added pressure did nothing to slow the take of the great fish. John spun the boat around in reverse, smacking right into a seven-foot swell, the spray reaching out and soaking me from head to toe. The cool sting of the salt water pimpled my skin and woke me up. This is what I had come all this way for. The stories written by Zane Grey about New Zealand that I read as a boy were coming to life in front of me. I felt the strength of the fish as I pushed against the footrest of the chair, straight-legged, head back, hands on top of the reel. The fish's power was fucking crippling. The reel hadn't stopped losing line since the hook came tight.

"Just let the fish run," Harry said, standing behind me. "We may be here awhile."

After a few minutes the fish slowed, and John tracked it from the helm, plowing through the growing swells. Fighting a giant fish is always a challenge. Fighting it in the middle of the night in the trough of a six- to eight-foot swell turns chest hairs white. One wrong move and the props could sever the line. Too fast in reverse and we could fill the cockpit with water, flooding the engine room or even sinking the boat. A clear head and a lifetime of experience is often overtaken by excitement and poor decision making. But not tonight. Not now.

"Talk to me, John," I yelled, holding the reel handle with my right hand, placing my left hand on top of the reel. I had learned years ago to use my lower body when battling fish from a fighting chair. Pulling on the rod with your arms and shoulders is not nearly as effective as using your legs, hips and body weight. I kept my legs straight, letting the power of the fish pull my ass a few inches off the seat. When I felt the opportunity, I'd swing my head back, lowering my body back to the chair and cranking in as much slack on the down stroke as I could. Up and down, losing more line than gaining. About half of the spool had vanished into the dark waters. God knows where. Out there, down there. Somewhere. Gone. I didn't let it discourage me.

"Tire yourself out," I said to the fish. "Pull, pull, pull. I ain't going anywhere."

"He's slowing down," John said. "I'm going to spin the boat and motor ahead. Parker, reel in any slack you can." John put one engine in forward and one in reverse to spin the boat, but the fish had other plans and fucking took off again. John stopped his spin, waiting for the fish's next move.

The waves were growing larger, the size of Volkswagen Beetles now. Cold seawater poured in over the covering boards at the corners of the transom as the boat pitched from port to starboard. Suddenly the rod tip started to rise, the rod straightening. My fears coming to life. Did he spit the hook?

"Reel!" Harry yelled. "Parker, reel. Hard! He's coming around." The captain eased the boat ahead. I cranked and cranked as fast as I ever had in my life. The fish was swimming directly at us now, and I knew that if I let the animal gain too much slack, the hook would fall free from the maw of the beast. My arm burned like glowing coals at the bottom of a campfire, but I turned and turned the reel handle as fast as I possibly could. The rod finally came tight, the slack back on the reel, and the chair swung to the left, the fish peeling off line again in yet another direction. The fish had rounded third base and was sprinting home.

"Good job Parker! Keep him tight," Harry said, patting me on my shoulder as he directed the fighting chair. "I think he'll settle down after this run."

"How long have we been hooked up?" I asked, thinking it was a good 30 or 45 minutes.

"Seventeen minutes," John answered.

"Fuck me." I said.

"I hope you packed a lunch, Parka," I heard someone mutter from behind me. It was Marvin. The fat man had appeared yet again, waving a lamb chop around like a conductor's baton. "Geez, John, how long you think it'll take this little pussy to catch a fish?"

"He's got a handle on it," John said nonchalantly. "Please clear the deck. It's getting nautical out here and I don't need you falling down."

"Me fall down? Who the fuck you think I am, some feather-footed faggot who's never been on a boat before?" Marvin said. "I caught four fah-king mahlin in a ..." He couldn't get his Tropic Star story out before a wave knocked into the boat beam-to, shuddering the entire hull. Marvin lost his balance. His feet flew out from underneath his gut, sending the big man across the deck on his belly like a seal on a slick beach. He crashed into a large icebox, rolled onto his hands and knees and crawled back toward the cabin door, the lamb chop dangling from his mouth. He yelled some gibberish at me as he crawled past the fighting chair.

"Nice move, Marvin," I said.

He spit out the chop, looked me dead in the eye and said, "Don't fuck this up, you fah-king pussy!"

It was just the motivation I needed. I let my ass rise out of the seat, the rod moving forward toward the water, reeling in a crank or two of line as the rod tip moved downward; then I threw my head back, sending my entire body back down to the chair, loading the rod again, tight against the fish. As the rod tip fell toward the ocean, I managed to get four cranks on the reel. I was starting to find my rhythm. Up and down, back and forward. Every inch counting more than ever. And so it went for a good hour. Inch by inch. I was holding my own against the fish, but hardly winning. The fish, I figured, had found the thermocline below the surface and was stalling out, regaining its strength from its long initial run. The thermocline is a demarcation zone under the surface of the ocean where the warmer surface waters give way to the colder deep water. The depth of the thermocline varies but the water below it holds more oxygen than the water above it. A fish parked under the thermocline can catch its breath and build its strength back after a long fight. I managed to reel in about one-third of the line that the fish had stolen off the reel. I also eased up the drag to impart more pressure against the mammoth being below.

The waves continued to grow. I felt my stomach drop more than once as the bow crested a large swell and fell down its backside. Marvin poked his head out of the cabin door a few times to mutter something at me, calling me a girl or a pussy. Little did he know that his insults were inspiring me to turn the handle and crank harder. Maybe he did know. Maybe he knew exactly what he was doing.

At some point Marvin became the official timekeeper. "Two hours, 30 minutes," he'd say. "You're such a fah-king little pussy. I would've caught this fish by now. C'mon Parka, you bitch." The door would shut. Harry would shake his head. Billy and I laughed. John remained silent.

Once you're in the fighting chair, locked into a big fish, there is no getting out until someone wins. It can go only one of two ways. You either beat the animal and manage to bring the fish to the side of the boat, or the fish wins and swims away freely. The odds are surely in the favor of the fish. There are hundreds of things that can go wrong for the angler, and often do. A knot or crimp breaks and the fish goes free. The hook pops out or snaps and the fish goes free. The reel seizes up and the line snaps. A shark appears and nicks the line or whacks your catch. The fish gets tail-wrapped and chafes through the line. So many scenarios can play out against the angler in the chair. But I didn't let myself think about any of that. All I could think of was how badly I wanted to see this fish. I wanted to see a New Zealand sword with my very own eyeballs. Its broad bill swinging like the sword of a black knight. I just wanted to see it. That was the goal. Bring the fish in and admire it. Maybe touch it with my own skin. My flesh against its golden dark flanks. I kept lifting and falling, cranking and pumping. It never got easier. Not one bit. At times, it felt like I had hooked the bottom and no matter how hard I pulled there was no breaking free.

The cabin door slid open a few inches. "Three hours, 45 minutes ... you fucking girl!"

By the fourth hour my will had diminished. My right hand throbbed. There was no opening the fingers, they were now molded into a claw wrapped firmly around the handle of the reel. My hips and lower back ached and burned. Each pump of the rod was more excruciating than the last. The waves continued to rise. Ten to 12-foot swells topped with whitecaps that licked at the boat with white foamy spittle.

"He must be getting tired by now, Parker," John said. "Push the drag up some."

I did as I was told, moving well past the strike button. My lower half felt the increased drag pressure. I started to use my arms more. Making smaller pumps and taking half-cranks with the reel handle. The big reel has two gears, high gear and low gear. High gear brings in more line with each crank but it's much tougher to spin the spool in high gear when you're tight to a large fish. I switched to low gear when I couldn't budge the animal in high gear. Back and forth. Inches of line decreasing to centimeters, but I'd take it. Accept it. Welcome each little bit of line I got back on the reel. Then the fish would swipe its tail a few times somewhere below and take the line back. We were sinking into a stalemate.

"You have to do something," I said to the crew. "I don't know how much more I've got."

John had already tried just about every trick he knew. He'd motored the boat up-sea. He'd tried surfing down-sea. Backing down on the animal in the rising waves was impossible unless we wanted to flood the boat.

The cabin door opened: "There's something wrong with the head," Marvin said.

"Not now!" John snapped and stomped his giant foot on the fiberglass floor of the flybridge. Marvin retreated.

"Hey Harry," John said, "you think it's dead?"

Harry looked up at his captain and shook his head no. "I just saw the rod tip bounce."

"Well, if we don't do something now, we won't ever catch this fish. I'm going to motor ahead. We'll probably lose a good bit of line, but my hope is the fish will start to plane up toward the surface. Once we get it up, I'll spin the boat and go down-sea as fast as we can and Parker will gain the line back. Ready the gaffs."

John eased the throttles up to trolling speed, pushing the boat up-sea, about six or seven knots, and I leaned back as far as my lower back would let me. I placed my hands on the sides of the coffee-can-size reel and watched the line I had worked so hard to gain disappear into the black ocean behind the boat.

"How much line we got?" the captain hollered.

"Half spool!" Harry yelled back.

"When it's down to a quarter, you let me know."

I clenched my teeth, the entire lower half of my body scorched from the pressure of the fish pulling against the drag, muscles burning like campfire embers. It felt like I was getting electrocuted from the inside out. Every tendon in my legs and lower back strained and shook. I kept my legs as straight as possible, with my shoulders and head far back, my eyes closed tightly, praying for it to end. But I wasn't going to give up.

"You can do this," Harry said in my ear, his head right next to mine. "When you feel John start to make his turn, I want you to get ready. Let your arms relax while you can because you're going to need them."

The boat plowed through the 10-foot seas, climbing some waves, smacking into others. I paid little attention to the ocean, or the sway and thud of the hull. Spray soared onto the deck, wetting my hair and face. I gritted my teeth. Harry wiped my face with a clean rag.

The cabin door slid open: "Hey Billy, are one of you guys going to come in and take a look at the head? I think it's pretty fucked up."

"Not now, Marvin! We're making our move on the fish. We'll deal with it later."

The fishing line kept rolling away. All that sweat. All that work. Four hours of fighting for inches — gone now. This move better work, I thought. No, it will work! It has to work. This is our last shot.

Harry placed his hand on my shoulder, shaking me, giving me a bro massage and trying to loosen me up for what he knew was ahead.

"Getting close John!" Harry yelled. Two more minutes ticked by. "Okay, now!"

John swung the bow of the boat into a wide spin so he wouldn't nick the fishing line, aiming the vessel down-sea and goosing the throttles to fight the hull's urge to surf down the growing swells. The captain worked the rudders to keep the boat in a quartering-sea position so we wouldn't get stuck in the throes of a full following sea, which would make it even harder to keep the bow straight as the waves pulled the boat back and flung it forward like a slingshot.

It was somewhere around two in the morning. The night sky was as dark as coffee. John was running on instinct, but a few clicks in the wrong direction and he'd run over the fishing line, severing all dreams I had of seeing this fish.

John pushed the throttles up, sending the bow of the boat crisscross into the 10- to 15-foot swells. Going up a large swell wasn't nearly as terrifying as coming down. I cranked in the slack as we worked our way down the waves, but my arms were turning to lead. I looked at Billy in a panic. He just shook his head, his hair soaked, water dripping down his chin. I had been so focused on the reel that I failed to realize the amount of water pouring into the cockpit from the ocean spray. The water was streaming down the gunwales like a river and raining off the top of the flybridge in a salty shower.

"You've got to reel, Parker. Just keep reeling," Billy said. He had the flying gaff in position. We must be getting close to actually catching this fish, I thought. The captain eased back on the throttles.

"Hang on!" John yelled. A massive rogue swell, as tall as a two-story building, knocked into the side of the boat, completely stopping the vessel for a brief second. Billy lost his footing and a wall of water sent him across the cockpit. I couldn't even reach out to try to help him. Both of my hands were too busy spinning the spool on the reel, fighting for line. Harry cracked open the tuna door in the transom to let some of the water drain out. I reeled. That was all I could do. I wanted to end this now more than ever. I was getting scared. The night felt darker than before. The seas were growing and growing like a mythical monster that slung saltwater fury.

John came off the bridge for a second to make sure we were all okay. He assured me that I was getting close, and he was right. The decision to go after the fish was a dangerous move but it was working. The line was coming in easier now. The stalemate had been lifted. It finally felt like we were winning the war. But the conditions were not making it easy. The boys had to clear the cockpit. Anything not tied down or stowed was sliding around like a hockey puck. I saw a 96-quart ice chest filled with hundreds of pounds of ice and drinks scoot across the deck like it weighed nothing at all.

My focus was broken by the most beautiful words I'd heard in days. "I see the double line!" Billy said. The double line marks the beginning of the end of a heavy-tackle fish fight. Crews double the last 10 to 20 feet of fishing line using a Bimini twist knot. This double line is connected to the final trace of heavy leader material via a swivel or wind-on leader, which is secured to the hook, usually with a crimp. We call it the end game.

Billy, the younger, stronger mate, put on his wiring gloves so he could grab hold of the leader and take wraps to pull the swordfish closer to the boat. I felt a shot of energy rattle through me and I let out a warrior cry. This fish was coming in. I had pumped and cranked, pumped and cranked. Gaining line. Losing line. Getting closer. Finally, there it was. Holy shit, this was the largest fish I'd ever seen attached to a fishing line. The animal moved across the sea behind the boat with remarkable speed. It was longer than the 13-foot beam of the boat. Its broad sword was a good six feet in length. My breath left me. I was amazed that I'd gotten this animal to the boat.

Madness exploded on deck.

Billy got low, crouching to bring his center of gravity down so he could pull against the fish. He was hanging on for dear life.

"Don't break the fucking line!" I yelled out. "Don't be a hero, Billy. Dump it if you need to."

He just shook his head. The fish turned back toward the boat. Billy managed to turn the big swordfish over. This fish was beat. It rolled onto its back and took a swipe of the tail, sending a wall of water onto all of us. What a joker. The swordfish was making a last effort to head back to the deep. It wanted to go home.

"We taking it or what?" John asked me.

"How big is it?" I responded.

"It's big, mate. I'd say 800-plus, conservatively. Biggest one I've seen in two years," John replied, much calmer than the mates who were bouncing from corner to corner as they worked the fish within gaffing range. Harry had the flying gaff in his hand. If we were to take this animal, Harry'd sink that gaff right behind the fish's giant head and pull hard enough to yank the gaff head off the aluminum pole and into the side of the fish. The gaff head is attached to rope that is either cleated off or tied to a big poly ball. Once that gaff sinks in, the fish is done for, unless it gets a surprise jolt of energy and takes off like a rocket. I've seen marlin take off so aggressively that the gaff pulls out. This fish was tired and far from green, but it was not dead.

"Try to get it alongside the boat," I said. "I'm putting my hands on that fish."

This animal looked like a dinosaur next to the boat, with a big sword sticking out of its head.

Harry put the gaff down and helped Billy as much as he could to position the fish so we could get a good look at it. The fish swung its sword a few times, like a dark knight fighting from his back. You can never count out a swordfish unless it's hanging by its tail from a gantry. The boys used their brawn, but gingerly moved the fish. They didn't want to piss it off.

Harry swung the fighting chair toward the fish. I eased the drag back and moved the rod to the holder on the side of the fighting chair so I could finally get out of the chair. The boat was in neutral and at the mercy of the ocean. It bobbed and bounced, making any movements on deck difficult. I slithered out of the chair onto the deck, my entire body spent. I didn't have the strength to combat the roll of the ocean. I got on my hands and knees and crawled to the side of the boat where it meets the transom. Billy was holding the leader just a few feet from the fish's mouth, but he wouldn't be able to hold it for long. The giant animal was right there, two feet off the starboard side. Its sheer size was mesmerizing. A monster. Hard to believe that something this big can swim with such power, speed and determination. I leaned over to see the swordfish up close, coming eye to eye with it. Its gallant sword swayed with the pitch of the boat. The fight within the beast was gone now. The fish was definitely dying on the line.

"Make a call, Parker!" John said.

I stuck my hand in the water and rubbed the side of the fish. The flanks of the fish were huge, about the width of a Clydesdale horse. My hand looked puny against its bronze back. Its eyeball, as large as a softball, stared at me. The dorsal fin stood a solid 20 inches tall. I was in awe. I had just reeled in a fucking elephant.

The tender moment between me and the swordfish did not last long.

"What the fahk are ya doing, Parka!" yelled Marvin, his head sticking out of the cabin door, spittle flying. "Take that fish! I want to hang it on my fah-king wall!"

I shook my head and looked at Harry, who had his camera in his hand.

"Say cheese," Harry said as he began to snap a bunch of photos. I managed to get up on one knee, like a tired football player, soaked to the bone, the energy drained out of every inch of my body but complete joy splattered across my face. Harry jumped around to snap photos from several angles, trying to get the entire fish in the frame, which was not easy because of the fish's length.

As I stared at the beast and reflected on its power and fight, I decided to let the animal swim away. To release it. This fish taught me what it means never to give up. This fish taught me what it means to set a goal and reach it. That was the object of this trip and I had accomplished my objective. I pulled Billy's knife out of its sheath on his safety belt, reached out toward my catch and cut the line. This fish could be defeated, but not destroyed. Not by me.

"Goodbye," I said. "You fought like a champion. You don't deserve to die just so some fat ass can hang you on his wall."

Harry put his arm around me, lifted me up to my feet and patted me on the back as he bear-hugged me. Marvin, however, went ballistic, jumping up and down like a two-year-old who had just dropped his ice-cream cone. I looked over the side of the boat, holding the covering board so I could watch the animal sink into the blackness. I never knew that I could reel in an animal like that. Anything is possible with the right gear and the right team.

The entire crew was completely wasted. The highs and lows had stolen whatever zeal we'd had. The fight lasted nearly six hours. The sun would rise soon. The date had changed. Another day was beginning. We were nearly 200 miles from our home port, a two-day steam, and the weather was getting worse by the minute. I was drenched, my hands pruned. I desperately needed a shower and dry clothes. Something to eat. A cold beer. My fight was over. It was time to go home.

The boys started to batten down the deck, returning the rods and reels and safely stowing all of the tackle. I didn't expect to hear a scream, but that's what shook me out of my contemplative mood.

"What the fuck?! What the fuck?!" someone yelled.

The words weren't used softly. They echoed off the cabin walls. There was pure panic in the words. Horror. My stomach sank. I thought we were sinking, but it was so much worse.

Billy flew out of the ship's cabin and raced up to the bridge.

"He shat up the whole fucking boat!" Billy shouted to John. "It's on the bloody ceiling, John. It's in my bunk!"

You have to understand that when men get together to go fishing for a few days, eating healthy is not of primary importance. Most meals on the boat are quick and filling. John's crew is different. They cook complete dinners with vegetables and rice, but there is no lack of snacks to break up the quiet moments. Chips, cookies, cheeses, sausages, sandwiches, frozen pizzas, copious amounts of beer, and anything microwavable is stocked with great abandon. Marvin had drained the cupboards nearly dry. Eventually it caught up to him and took the rear exit.

At some point during the six-hour swordfish battle, old Marvin's bowels began to constrain and bulge, desperately needing to release all that saturated fat and congealed meat. He'd made it to the bowl, but with the growing swell and pitching boat, his balance was thrown off. He had to hang on to keep his cheeks planted on the seat. He must've been gripping the toilet somewhere right below the bowl, where it narrowed and connected to the base. Physics eventually took over. Marvin's mass proved too much for the poor bowl, and it died a miserable death. The porcelain broke right at the foundation, severing the toilet from the rest of the head and creating an opening for an explosive shit geyser to shoot out and flow into the boat.

We'd been at sea for days, with four grown men eating three-plus solid meals a day. The holding tank was full — "was" being the key word. The scene was horrific. Ankle-deep shit water in the staterooms down below. The stench hit me hard when I stepped inside to view the scene, taking away my breath and instantly gagging me like a doctor with a popsicle stick.

John went down to investigate. I think I heard him whimper a little bit. The Toilet Paper King of Manhattan had destroyed the throne. There was some tragic irony there for sure, but I was not about to mention it. I was too scared, wondering what the powerful captain might do. The mates were full-chested and spitting fire. This boat is their home. Their workplace.

I snuck off, fearing a bloody scene, and braced myself on the deck of the boat, trying to hide behind the bridge ladder.

The captain didn't say a word as he assessed the damage. He shook his head, completely dismayed.

"I told the crew the head was fucked up," Marvin said, sitting on the couch as if nothing had happened.

"Fucked up?" John responded. "You snapped it off the fucking base, Marvin! My entire boat is filled with shit."

"That's what you get for having a cheap toilet," Marvin said.

A very bad choice of words.

John grabbed Marvin around the neck. The mates tried to pull John off Marvin's jugular, but it was no use. John was frantic. He dragged the fat man to the head and stuck Marvin's big bald melon right into the shit water, like he was training a puppy who'd just peed on the living-room rug. Marvin tried to scream, which was another bad decision because before you can scream, you must suck in a lot of air, or, in this case, shit water. Harry retreated to the deck and pushed up against me in the corner. We were about as far away from the scene as you could get. Billy stayed, a good soldier backing up his captain.

"Is he going to drown him in his own shit?" I asked Harry, who had started to laugh uncontrollably. "This is serious, man. He's going to kill him!"

At some point, John's senses came over him and he loosened his grip on Marvin, but the torture for this paying client was far from over. There were no police out here. No rules, and Marvin was vastly outnumbered.

The crew pumped out whatever feces was left in the holding tank and shoved a bunch of rags in the toilet hole to plug it. They cleaned up the cabin and staterooms as best they could with buckets of Simple Green. Unfortunately, conditions were too rough to open the hatches and air things out as we were motored home. No one spoke to Marvin. Not a word. Two hundred miles to steam back to the dock. The run took more than 20 hours. Marvin became invisible and it tortured him. He tried to spark up conversations with all of us, but no one played along.

"Ay, Parka, you going to get a mount of that fish?"

Did someone say something? I don't think so ...

The big man's New York accent was like a tree falling in some forgotten woods. Nobody heard it.

The rest of us enjoyed our time away from Marvin. The mood lightened and we swapped stories. We ate like civilized adults, with no one there to spit food at us while they devoured a meal like a ravenous teenager trying to talk, eat and laugh at the same time.

John berthed the boat at Bay of Islands and I departed with little fanfare as I often do. I gave the crew a big tip and told them that I would be back one day. Marvin did his best to sneak out and dodge the bill. A month or two later, Marvin's credit card was hit with a boatyard bill to install a new head, replace the floors and update all of the upholstery on the boat. More than 15 grand I'd guess, but I'm not sure. The Toilet Paper King never made his way back to New Zealand.

CHAPTER EIGHT

Sandbaggers

Sandbagger: n. A person who downplays or misrepresents his or her ability in an effort to deceive, cheat or obtain the upper hand, especially in gambling, or in this case, fishing.

"Are you really sure you want to do this?" I asked.

"Yes!" Capt. Teddy Griffin responded emphatically.

"Seriously, Teddy, I think you're going a bit too far with all of this," I said.

"I'll tell you what's too far, mate. Those motherfuckers have been using our intel for weeks and never shared a goddamn bite. So I'm going to fill this bag with sand, and I'm going to make a statement."

Teddy's knees were freckled with bits of crushed rock as he shoveled handfuls of the white Caribbean granules into a plastic zipper bag. He looked ridiculous. A grown man frantically taking handfuls of sand and smashing them into a bag the size of a throw pillow, compacting the grit with a mix of rage and madness. Beads of sweat popped up on his shaved head like condensation on a cold cocktail. He muttered awful thoughts under his breath with discernible phrases like "going to kill" and "maim you" rising to the top of the cauldron.

The shoveling continued until the gallon-size bag was full like a stuffed bear. Teddy held the bag up and grinned at me with an uneasy, teeth-showing half smile.

"You look fucking crazy, man. Maybe you should just take a breath and rethink this for a second."

"Nah, all good mate," Teddy said, a menacing gleam to his wide, ice-blue eyes. "Let's bloody do this!"

He popped up to his bare feet and launched into a high-speed march back toward the marina. I could hardly keep up with him.

"Slow down!" I hollered as he strode farther away from me.

"Teddy. Teddy!"

There was no halt to Teddy's gait. I struggled to keep within five strides of him. The veins on his forearms and neck were enlarged, pumped up and fueled with a fury I'd never seen in him before.

He flew down the ramp to C dock, his march quickening with each step. He was a couple pumps shy of jogging. I picked up my stride, fearing a fight. I spotted a fillet knife on a bait table behind one of the boats on the dock and snatched it up as I motored past, holding it against my leg. Jesus, Teddy, please don't go nuts, I thought to myself.

Teddy got to *Ambitious* about 20 seconds before me. He jumped off the bulkhead dock and landed right on the teak deck of the cockpit four feet below, causing a massive boom that I'm sure rattled everyone inside the boat like a cannonball fired from a galleon. In a flash Teddy was standing at the salon door, the bag of sand in his right hand. His left hand was clenched into a tight fist that he used to knock on the door. Not a soft knock. It was a full-on cop knock. Bang! Bang! Bang!

The door to the 70-foot sportfishing yacht slowly slid open, gliding gracefully along its track, powered by a hydraulic ram operated by a button.

"What the fuck, Teddy?!" screamed the man who opened the door. He was in his twenties, tall, tan and in very good shape. But he was scared. You could tell from his pained squint and shaking hands that he was not about to fall on any sword.

"May I please come in?" Teddy asked, his best schoolboy smile smugly plastered across his face.

"No, you may not. The boss is on the phone, and he doesn't much appreciate you scaring the shit out of everyone." This was about when I got to the boat and quietly stepped onto the deck. I stood two feet behind Teddy, panting like an overweight Labrador retriever.

"It will only take a second," Teddy said and pushed the young man aside. The deckhand didn't push back. The owner of the boat, a wealthy banker from Brazil, was sitting at the dinette table, speaking Portuguese into a cell phone. He wore his long white hair slicked back and tied in a tight ponytail. He had on a long-sleeve shirt with the name of the boat, *Ambitious*, and a drawing of the boat on the front pocket. A thick gold chain hung around his neck outside of his shirt. I didn't know his name. He was a new player on the offshore tournament circuit. For his first boat he purchased a 70-foot production yacht-fisher that probably cost about $3.2 million. He hired a crew to take care of it and put him on fish. All he did was order guys around and reel in whatever they could hook. Unfortunately for the crew, the owner preferred to fish alone. He was ultra-competitive.

The owner held his hand up to Teddy like you might do to someone you want to high-five, but this slick character didn't want to slap hands. He was using his hand like a crossing guard, telling Teddy to stop. The man was too engrossed in his phone call, or didn't want to show Teddy the respect to end the call. Across the dinette from the boat's owner sat the captain, a 30-something guy that everyone called Beans. The captain knew that Teddy was here to see him, and he didn't make eye contact with Teddy. Teddy had no interest in talking to the owner or the deckhand. Teddy got right in the captain's face. Their noses were two or three inches apart. I'm sure Beans could smell Teddy's sweat and feel his breath against his chin.

"Don't you ever call me on the fucking radio again unless you're fucking sinking," Teddy said. His words came out slowly and deliberately with just a hint of his Australian accent. Teddy bit down on every syllable, the corners of his jaw moving like he had a mouthful of marbles. Teddy lifted the bag of sand high above his head and held it there until everyone in the room was staring at it. Then he opened his grip and let the sandbag drop onto the table. Thunk. The bag didn't open or pop, but the message was delivered. The captain's mouth fell open and he gasped. The deckhand froze, wide-eyed. The owner went quiet and pulled his phone away from his ear. Teddy stepped backward out of the salon, his gaze fixed on Beans. Teddy smiled the whole way out of the boat.

There are not many rules in the sport of offshore fishing, but a code of conduct does exist. These ethics are not written down in any journal or book, but if you spend enough time fishing, you get a sense of the unspoken best practices and can quickly tell the good crews from the bad.

Much like sandbox rules, there is a way to play nice and then there is everything else. You're going to have to share from time to time. You're going to have to help one another. Don't steal. Don't lie. Play fair and you will be liked wherever you go. If you don't adhere to the rules, the word will get out and you may find yourself in a strange port somewhere with a major boat problem and nobody willing to help you. It always comes back around. As for Beans, the shit was all over the fan. He'd pissed off one of the good guys who had a big network of other good guys.

For many men, fishing is an ego thing, and for these particular men, just about everything is an ego thing. I generally despise these guys. The amount of pressure they put on themselves and everyone around them is infectious — in a bad way. Like the measles. We all prefer to win over losing, but there are various ways to go about it. We're all inherently competitive. We like the feeling of catching the most fish or the biggest one on the dock. Sometimes it is only pure luck that separates the winners from the runners-up. But more often than not, the winners did their homework, they prepared, left nothing to chance and were rewarded for their efforts.

For a fisherman, pulling into the marina as the day's high hook is akin to winning the "big" game, especially in one of the major fishing hot spots like Hatteras, Montauk, Orange Beach, St. Thomas, Cabo or Isla. If you've been lucky enough to fish one of those spots, or one similar, then you know the caliber of the crews that tie up there. Beating the best captains and crews in the world makes winning even more triumphant. It's no fun to beat up on the newbies. That's easy, but out-fishing someone you respect is pretty spectacular.

Pick your favorite sport to play: football, baseball, tennis or golf — it really doesn't matter. Think about the day you played your best. The day you beat your rival. That memory lives on inside of you. It's the same thing for anglers, especially when fishing tournaments.

While I'm not a huge tournament guy, Teddy is. He's also a professional captain who owns his own vessel and does all of his own marketing. To him, winning a tournament equates to a nice chunk of money in his pocket and generates some buzz about him through social media and the local coconut wire (aka dock talk). Teddy has won plenty of tournaments because of his preparations. He checks and rechecks all of his tackle. He goes through the boat meticulously to make sure all systems are perfect. And when he wins, he's not a dick about it. He doesn't talk shit. Sure, Teddy likes to bust balls and light a few fires, but he abides by the unspoken code. For that reason, Teddy resides in the circle of trust. The same cannot be said for Capt. Raymond "Beans" Diaz, a transplanted Puerto Rican guy who got his nickname as a teenager working on the charter boats out of Hillsboro Inlet in South Florida. Some captain he worked for thought Beans was Mexican, even when Raymond explained over and over that he was Puerto Rican, and a U.S. citizen. The name stuck. I didn't know him before flying down to the Caribbean to fish with Teddy, but I'd heard about him.

Turns out Beans and Teddy had some history. For the past several years the two men fished the Caribbean during the summer, mostly trolling for blue marlin and white marlin from St. Thomas in the U.S. Virgin Islands. They ran into each other at a tournament or two in Puerto Rico, and both crews fished the final six weeks of the summer blue marlin bite in the Dominican Republic, fishing the FADs (fish-aggregating devices) stationed along the southern coast.

There were only 12 or so full-time offshore fishing boats operating out of Punta Cana in the D.R. for the months of May and June, when the bite is typically the best. And they all ported in the same marina. A small community, no doubt, with a lot of ocean to cover. The crews hung out together at the marina bar, and the captains touched base on the VHF radio throughout the day. Some captains worked more closely together than others, but for the most part information was shared openly. Boats that work together inevitably catch more fish. They can cover more water, try different techniques and figure out patterns to determine what baits or teasers are working better in particular conditions.

Radio chatter is a way for guys to cut through the boredom in between bites. But it's not just senseless riling. These captains are mining for intel. Captains have their own ways of pulling information out of one another. Sometimes they're direct: "What'd you catch over there?" Other times it's more like banter.

"*Reel Affair, Reel Affair,* you on here, Billy?"

"I gotcha, Teddy, what's up?"

"Slow morning, mate," Teddy says, his Aussie accent giving him away. "Been fishing Two Rocks. Got one bite early on but it didn't come tight. Small white marlin. Where you at, Billy?"

"Roger that, buddy. We ran out to the FADs. Bite just started to pick up. Just released our second blue."

"Hey, there ya go. If you catch one with a blue Hawaiian Eye in its face, that's mine," Teddy says. "Lost one out there a couple days ago."

"I'll keep an eye out for it, Teddy. Good luck today."

"You too, Billy. If it turns on here, I'll let you know."

"Roger that, appreciate it."

Now both guys knew what was going on at the other spot. No burning intel, just a few tips. If it did turn on, they may let each other know. Or they may not. But if you do share that kind of burning-hot information, telling the other boat to make a five- or 10-mile run because the bite is going Richter, well then you expect to receive the same kind of information down the road. It's a reciprocal thing. If you only take and never give, you end up with a bag of sand on your salon table, an upset boss and a bad reputation.

"Don't take another step, you fucking Aussie coward!" Beans yelled at Teddy and me as we were laughing our way back to the boat. Teddy stopped and turned, his signature smile shining brightly. He opened up his arms like the crucifix and didn't say a word. I instantly regretted my decision to return the fillet knife I pocketed earlier.

Beans was carrying the bag of sand. When he was about 15 feet away from us, he lifted his left leg like a baseball pitcher and hurled the bag of sand using all of his body weight. His rear leg came off the ground as he let the bag fly, sending it whizzing over Teddy's head by a good three feet. The bag smashed into a shore-power utility box, knocking off a big chunk of the white plastic covering. The zipper of the bag opened and white sand spilled out onto the concrete bulkhead.

Teddy didn't move an inch. "Nice throw, Beans," he said. I couldn't help but laugh. Beans' entire face was bright red. He was raging mad, huffing and puffing like the big bad wolf. But he wasn't that big, nor that bad. Teddy folded his arms and stood his ground. The two men looked like they were about to have an old-fashioned duel, facing one another from a distance of 20 paces. I was waiting for one of them to reach for their weapon, but they were both wearing board shorts, T-shirts and flip-flops.

"Don't you ever fucking jump on my boat again, you got me," Beans said, some foam forming at the corners of his dark lips. His eyes were shielded behind dark, wraparound shades. His hair was jet black and set in place with gel that made it look wet.

"I don't plan on it, you fucking idiot," Teddy said. "You know what you did. For days you call me on the radio and ask how they're biting. I give you honest information of where and when we caught fish. You don't give me shit, and then at the end of the day I hear that you caught three or four fish. You are a fucking sandbagger and I don't want shit to do with you."

"I'm in the fucking tower all day, man," Beans said. "Maybe the radio isn't sending out as good as it's picking up. I don't know. I'm fishing the FADs 50 miles from you."

Teddy looked at me. I shook my head 'no.' Beans runs a $3 million boat. The radio worked fine. We heard him throughout the day, doing the same shit to the other captains in the area. He was trying to bullshit his way out of this.

The captains and mates on the other boats started assembling in the cockpits of their vessels, hoping to see something entertaining. Other than fishing, life gets kind of stagnant at this particular marina. Finally, there was something good to watch.

"Hey Billy," Teddy hollered to Capt. Billy Whitman who was

sitting on a cooler in the cockpit of *Reel Affair*, a gorgeous 60-foot Carolina custom sport-fisher with a flared bow and teak toe rail. He was drinking a rum cocktail out of a red plastic cup, enjoying this little debate.

"Billy, when was the last time Beans asked you how they were biting?"

"Yesterday."

"And did you give some information on the fish you'd seen?"

"Sure I did," Billy said. "That's how us North Carolina boys do things. We are a very sharing, caring people."

"Did Beans reciprocate?"

"Fuck no," Billy said. "When I saw his mate at the bar that night, I said if he ever calls me on the radio again I'd have to tell him to go fuck a sheep."

"What about that time I gave you a few dozen ballyhoo, Billy?" Beans said. "You saying you'll take my bait but you won't be a Carolina gentleman?"

Old Billy didn't like that comment one bit. He took a gulp from his drink, put it down on the covering board and stood up. Billy was pushing 50, but he had gone to school at Duke and played defensive end. He certainly hadn't forgotten how to hurt a man. Billy slowly stepped from his boat onto the dock and started to walk toward Beans.

"All right, all right, you guys made your point," Beans said, holding up his hands. "This is stupid. From this point on I am going to announce all of my hookups over the radio, okay? I'll tell you the GPS coordinates for each bite. Fuck, I'm going to tell you guys when I fart, when I shit and what I'm eating for lunch. Sound good? Happy now?"

"Maybe you should just go back to Mexico, Señor Beans," Billy said, accentuating his Carolina drawl.

Beans took the walk of shame back toward his boat. His sinewy 20-year-old mate lingered a good 50 feet away from him, talking to one of the deckhands from another boat.

"Thanks a lot for backing me up, Sean!" Beans hollered at the kid. Sean just looked at the ground. When Beans was out of earshot, Sean called him a pussy. The young man then came over to me, Teddy and Billy.

"You have no idea how much it sucks working for him," Sean said. "He and the boss hardly get along, and the entire vibe on the boat is all business and no fun. They don't play any music. There is no beer on the boat. When the bite is good, it's somewhat tolerable, but I'm going fucking nuts, man."

"Sounds like you're looking for a job," Billy said to the young man. "You don't want to work for a captain like that. He'll only teach you how to do things the easy way, which is usually the wrong way."

In an effort to assuage future dockside shenanigans, I have taken the liberty of constructing some basic rules for fishermen to abide by. So let it be said that the unwritten rules are now written. Forgive me if I sound a bit preachy.

The Ten Commandments of Fishing

1- Don't Be a Dick: I claim this rule to be self-evident.

2- Never Leave a Boat in Need: Always, always, always respond to emergencies at sea. If you see a dead boat, make an effort to help out. It is Mariner's Law. What goes around comes around.

3- Thou Shalt Not Steal Another Man's Spot: Don't be that guy. A fisherman's GPS waypoints and unmarked hot spots are sacred property. We spend thousands of hours on the water and obscene amounts of money to accumulate a log full of fishing spots. Yes, you can cruise right by and grab my numbers, but I say shame on you.

4- Don't Cheat and Don't Lie: All fishermen exaggerate the truth at times, but don't lie. Don't cheat in tournaments. Don't shove weights down the belly of a fish you're about to place on a scale. It makes us all look bad.

5- Maintain a Wide Berth When Someone is Hooked Up: Nothing is more frustrating than another boat motoring over to you as you're fighting a fish. I've seen people try to run over each other's lines in big-money tournaments to cut off a potential winning fish. People like that deserve a jellyfish sting down below.

6- Respect the Locals: Every location has its own way of doing things. Be friendly and courteous when you arrive to fish a new spot. Help the locals. Gain their respect and you will be rewarded. Treat them like dog shit, and you'll end up like Captain Cook ... who was murdered.

7- Don't Covet Thy Neighbor's Boat: It's not the size of the boat that matters ...

8- Don't Covet Thy Neighbor's Mate: This one has a fair bit of gray area, but you shouldn't make a habit of stealing good deckhands from others. If they come to you on their own, well, that's a little bit different.

9- Own Up to Your Mistakes: If you break something on the boat, be honest about it and either pay to get it fixed or roll up your sleeves and do it yourself. If you screw up and miss a fish, expect to be mocked. Take it like a champ. It happens to all of us.

10- Have Fun: It's fishing. Not school. Not work. If you're not having fun, you aren't doing it right.

CHAPTER NINE

Marlin Punch

I first met Capt. Jeff Quinn on the crowded floor of the Miami Beach Convention Center during the Miami International Boat Show, one of the largest in the world. Many of the big names in the sportfishing world show up each year to conduct business, sign sponsors, talk smack and uncoil a bit.

The 20-something Quinn quickly made a name for himself, pissing off some of the older, leather-skinned curmudgeonly captains with loud accusations and arrogant claims that he'd out-fish any one of them on any ocean.

Quinn's young, fit and energetic exterior gave him some suaveness with the ladies. He'd walk booth to booth, showing off the blond on his arm and the photos of cow-size yellowfin tuna on his phone. The young captain was completely obsessed with himself, as most young guns are, but he had some proof in his pudding. He lived and breathed the sport — the kind of person who would wake up at three a.m. to go catch an early morning bite before anyone else even blinked a crusty eyelid. And he'd do his homework. Studying the currents, ocean temperatures and moon phases. When he surmised that the bite was really good, he wouldn't be able to sleep at all and would get out to the fishing grounds even earlier.

I liked his swagger.

We met up for drinks that evening at the Clevelander, a super-loud, techno-blasting booze joint located on South Beach's otherwise posh stretch of eateries and clubs along Ocean Drive. The beers flowed freely as Quinn told fish story after fish story, using wild hand motions and sound effects to keep me engrossed. He'd hang onto an imaginary fishing rod — left hand on the rod, right hand on the reel, bouncing around as he described the pull of a big yellowfin tuna and the effort needed to get the reel handle to crank over. I ate it up and shared a few tales of my own.

Quinn grew up in a fishing family in British Columbia, Canada. As he got older and times got tougher, he dropped out of school and started fishing full time, mostly for salmon, to help support his family. If there wasn't a charter, he'd jump on his uncle's commercial boat and go out hoping for a big haul and an even bigger payday. He eventually started his own charter business, all before the age of 20, and it didn't take long for his fishing prowess to gain attention. He specialized in catching king salmon up north, but his ego and drive required bigger fish to feed his fantasy of becoming the biggest name in the fishing world.

Quinn drove all the way down the Pacific coast from Canada to Puerto Vallarta, Mexico, where a friend told him the marlin and tuna fishing was untapped and "off the hook." The trip turned into a five-week fishing marathon punctuated with a 325-pound beast of a yellowfin tuna. The kind of fish that will have you praying to the unholy gods for the line to break as your back burns and your arms go numb from overexerting your limits. No man is made to go toe to toe with a 300-plus-pound tuna. Except maybe Quinn. He ate the shit up. The following year he trailered a 26-foot Grady-White sportfishing boat nearly 2,300 miles, from British Columbia down to Puerto Vallarta to run charters. He didn't speak Spanish, knew only a few people in town and had no slip space rented. He just rolled the dice and hit the road.

It didn't take him long to figure out the fishery and advance the techniques and tactics used by the local fleet. He'd fly kites and run baits off a kite line, making them skip across the surface like a stunned piece of candy dancing in front of the massive predators this area is known for.

Word got out quickly as his photos of big fish were picked up and featured in several West Coast fishing magazines, his tanned torso standing next to a giant yellowfin tuna, the fish upside down on the deck of the boat, with its tail up over Quinn's head. His tattoos blazed in the sun as his finely cut arms wrapped around the midsection of a tuna so big that he'd have to stand the animal on its face and stand next to it to accurately portray the animal's size. Lifting its 300-pound load was completely out of the question, even for this crazy Canadian.

The photos worked wonders for the young gun's reputation. Stories circulated through the coconut wire as Quinn became known for doing whatever it took to find a fish. As he ascended in the sport, so did his bookings. Known for wild fishing and unconscionable behavior, Quinn attracted a certain clientele — guys who liked to party just as hard as they fished.

We stayed in touch after that first meeting, and I often found myself drooling over the photos Quinn would email me from Mexico. This kid knew what we anglers wanted to see. Big fish, hot women and long days on the water filled with action.

I finally planned a trip after a couple of years of persistent invitations. I flew down to Puerto Vallarta in July to coincide with some of the best marlin and tuna action of the year. We hoped to catch cow-size yellowfin tuna on the kite baits and pull some lures for blue and black marlin.

Quinn met me at the airport in Puerto Vallarta with the requisite beer in one hand and two half-drunk bikini models in tow.

"What's up, you old sack of goat nuts?" he said, his smile running up to each lens of his mirrored sunglasses.

We were off to a solid start.

Puerto Vallarta is one of only a few natural harbors on mainland Mexico's Pacific coast. The large body of water, known as Banderas Bay, provides safe shelter from any big winds or hurricanes that rumble up the coast. The marina here is home to several private big-game fishing outfits as well as a handful of world-class charter operators. Quinn sort of lives in between both worlds, running private boats and offering charters on his smaller, outboard-powered craft.

After a short ride from the airport to the harbor, we jumped on *Intimidator*, a 40-foot Cabo express sportfishing vessel docked at Marina Vallarta. Quinn didn't own the boat, but he sure acted like he did. He insisted that the ladies, if I could call them that, remove their stiletto heels before stepping on the boat. Heels can do more damage to the fit and finish on a boat than an oil leak.

A wealthy broker from Chicago owned the vessel, and Quinn

was on retainer to run it for him. When the owner wasn't around, Quinn kept the boat in fishing condition — that meant going out whenever possible. A sitting boat is an unhappy one. We motored out of the harbor and headed to Punta Mita on the northern tip of the bay, much closer to the fishing action.

Every summer, huge congregations of skipjack tuna stack up around Corbeteña Rock, some 15 miles off the beaches of Punta Mita. The offshore fishing action also blows up farther out around El Banco, a large seamount, where the depths shoot up from 2,000 feet to less than 300. The abundance of skipjack tuna and mackerel attracts apex predators such as blue and black marlin, gigantic yellowfin tuna and all manner of massive sharks.

Quinn had been running charters out of the Puerto Vallarta area for several years now. Unlike most local charter boats that base their operations out of Marina Vallarta, Quinn prefers the more laid-back, charming village of Punta Mita. But it's not Punta Mita's charm that Quinn really likes — it's the closer run to the offshore grounds.

While it's the yellowfin tuna that helped him build his reputation, the blue marlin curdled his blood and fired up his spirit.

"We focused on tuna so much in the first few years I was down here that we really didn't realize we had an unbelievable black and blue marlin fishery," he told me. "I think we've barely scratched the surface. Each day out there we learn more about the marlin fishery. These fish haunt my sleep and push me to get out on the fucking water every chance I get. It's kind of like the first time I tasted pussy."

I wasn't about to deprive the guy of that.

"I could catch tuna off the kite baits all day, but I'd take a blue marlin over a tuna," said the cocksure captain. We switched up tactics and decided to go after the big man in the blue suit.

Banderas Bay acts as a year-round nursery for baitfish. Couple that with the favorable geography found offshore — reefs, islands, natural marine reserves, banks and nearly bottomless canyons — and you've got the ideal setting for outstanding fishing. Lay all that structure down in an already productive migratory and spawning corridor for big-game fish and you have a recipe for serious offshore debauchery.

We decided to employ two different tactics — fishing with live skipjack tuna and trolling custom lures. Tuna, which have extremely keen eyesight, can see heavy leaders used at the end of the line when pulling lures. Since we decided to go after some marlin on this trip, we elected to use thick, durable, 500-pound monofilament leaders when trolling our large marlin lures, about the size of a man's forearm. The tuna won't go near this thick stuff unless they're really famished or just in an ornery mood. The thick leaders will also keep the marlin from gnawing through and breaking off.

We fished from dawn to dusk on our first day, raising four blue marlin in the 300-pound range and getting two solid hookups. Both fish came unbuttoned, spitting the hook after a series of jumps. We weren't disheartened. If anything, seeing those marlin got us rolling. Few sights in the natural world compare to a fierce, wild-eyed blue marlin as it kicks the ocean into a white, foamy mess, slinging itself across the surface in a frantic dance of madness. They'll appear behind the spread of trolling lures, fast as bullets, and lit up with colors you've only ever seen on a Vegas marquee. Bright flashes, blue stripes and swaths of purple move through the water like lightning, zipping from one lure to the next as the fish picks its prey. Sometimes the fish torpedo themselves straight up from the depths, much like a raising submarine. The water will explode where the lure once was as the giant fish whacks its baseball bat of a bill at it. And when they can't figure out why the prey won't die, they just get more aggressive. More angry. More colorful. More fun.

When you're lucky enough to hook a blue marlin, you need to settle in and get ready for a fight. This usually isn't a one-round knockout. It's a 12-round slugfest.

Just prior to my arrival, Quinn and his crew released 12 marlin in one day! That's the sort of stuff big-game fishing dreams are made of. We knew the billfish were here. We felt their presence. The air was thick with the pungent smell of bait. I was sure one of these denizens had just decimated a school of skipjack tuna somewhere nearby.

I stood next to the fishing rod running up to the outrigger, the lure bubbling along in the left-long position in the spread behind the boat. I watched the lure, the farthest in the spread, skitter across the top of the waves. It looked good enough to eat, and I knew it wouldn't take long for an ol' blue to show up. But it wasn't a blue dog that showed up at all.

On the second day of our trip, a 250-pound black marlin broke the ice, plowing onto a chugger-head lure and began to run line off the reel like someone had forgotten to set the drag. I pulled the bent-over rod out of the holder, the reel singing as the fish continued to burn off line and headed for Cabo San Lucas some 300 miles west. Pushing the drag lever up on the reel, I came tight to the fish, and the marlin sling-shotted itself clear out of the water like it'd just been electrocuted. Quinn shouted something from his perch in the tuna tower, where he piloted the boat. He was standing with his back to the bow, eyes focused on the action behind the stern, an engine throttle in each hand. His eyes were glued on the fish as he swung the boat around to give chase and gain back some line.

I placed the gimbal at the bottom of the rod butt snuggly in my fighting belt and felt it lock into the place. I secured the stand-up harness around my lower back and hips, and clicked the carabiner from the harness onto the lugs on the top of the reel. With this gear, I could battle the fish standing up, using my body weight and legs to lift the rod and put pressure against the fish that was acting like a bumper car driven by a drunk girl on the Jersey Shore.

The fish flipped behind the boat, tail-walking across the surface, displaying its beautiful colors. Its dorsal fin stood as erectly as a porn star as the fish gave a few head shakes, trying to break free. The fish mostly stayed on the surface and Quinn chased it down quickly. In about 30 minutes, I had my first Pacific black marlin next to the boat. The mate, a displaced Southern California surfer dude named Brad, took hold of the leader, wrapping his hands around the mono and yanking on the fish like a lumberjack sawing down a tree. I backed off on the drag to release the pressure on the line and made my way to the starboard covering board to get a good look at the fish. The marlin was tired but still feisty. I removed the rod from the belt and harness so I could reach down and touch the bill. I patted the fish on the head as Brad worked the hook loose and set the marlin free.

Soon after that first marlin, Quinn rattled something off in Spanish, and the second mate, a local kid named Pico, snapped into motion and began digging through the tackle drawer. He came out with an odd trolling lure. It had a purple slanted head with yellow flanks and a long, yellow-under-purple skirt. Pico held the lure up to Quinn on the bridge.

"Oh yeah, baby!" he said. "That's the game changer. We've never used that color combination. I came up with it last night when I was lapping tequila shots out of Shannon's belly button. I put it together around two this morning."

"Who's Shannon?" I asked.

"Got me, mother fucker!" he yelled out. It was the same response he always used when someone asked him about a girl. Good practice, really. You never know ... you could be talking to her boyfriend, or worse, her father.

"You're insane, you know that, right?" I said.

"Deranged!" he screamed.

Pico expertly rigged the lure up with a single 10/0 hook, making sure to leave the bend of the hook exposed and free from the lure's skirt material. Quinn swears you hook just as many fish using a single hook as opposed to rigging the lure with tandem hooks. And when you're running singles you don't run as high of a risk of foul-hooking the fish as you do with doubles.

Pico dropped the lure in the prop wash behind the boat and set it out to my favorite position, the left short.

We were running just five lures. Two lures placed about seven waves back behind the boat in the wake, one on each side. Two other lures were run close to the corners of the transom, just two waves back. The fifth lure, a jet head that ran straight as a ruler, was set straight down the middle. Quinn calls this one the "WTFB," the Way the Fuck Back lure. Some guys call it a shotgun. We also had two hookless teasers manned by the madman up in the tower. A giant lure made by Mold Craft called the Enormous

Johnson chugged along on one side, and a big custom lure made by Capt. Black Bart threw a bubble trail on the other side. If there was a big marlin hunting nearby, it would want to investigate this spread of commotion.

About an hour later, the game changer produced the eruption Quinn was looking for. A nice marlin surfaced behind the lure, lifting its head out of the water like a sea monster. Mouth opened, it pounced on the game changer in a splash of white water, chewing on the hunk of plastic as if it were a gummy bear stuck in its molar. The hook dug in deep. This fish wasn't getting off.

But instead of jumping and going ballistic upon the hookup like most blue marlin do, the fish sort of stayed in one spot, slashing its bill back and forth like a windshield wiper. Quinn, who got the best view of the fish high above the action in the boat's tuna tower, originally called it a black marlin because of the way it was fighting. Whatever species it was, we didn't care. I took the rod out of the holder and stood next to the fighting chair. The fish didn't have that initial burst of pandemoniac energy typical of a blue marlin. My instincts told me it'd be a long, drawn-out fight. I hopped in the chair, set the rod butt in the gimbal and attached the bucket harness to the reel.

The fish made one halfhearted jump in the early stages of the battle, and we gained line rather easily. Too easy. We had her alongside *Intimidator* in just 15 or 20 minutes and Quinn hadn't yet stopped his aggressive maneuvers with the boat. The waves poured over the stern as we smacked into the green water going six or seven knots in reverse. The transom cavitated each time it slapped into one of the swells covered in surface chop. The waves were dimpled, and as the winds picked up, they began to turn white and frothy.

The captain hollered at the marlin. Insulting it, calling the fish a pussy and threatening it to put up a fight.

"You're better than that!" he yelled. "Show me your colors!"

Just as Brad reached out to grab the leader so he could pull the fish closer to the boat and get the hook out for a safe release, the fish's true colors became frighteningly apparent. Its temperament switched on like a prize fighter against the ropes who had just gotten his final shot of adrenaline. The warrior within the lame-duck marlin woke the fuck up.

Brad took a wrap on the thick monofilament with a gloved hand, but he couldn't hang on. The fish sprinted away from him, causing him to open his hand and dump the leader. Just as he let go of the line, the fish reappeared off the starboard side of the boat and made a jump toward the sun.

The 350-pound blue marlin shot straight out of the water, launching its entire body, all seven feet of it, clear out of the choppy sea.

The fish's wide, V-shaped tail acts like a jet engine, making the blue marlin one of the fastest-swimming creatures in the ocean. And this fish had switched on its afterburners.

As the leaping marlin reached the apex of its jump, the fish turned upside down, arcing like a rainbow, and came straight at me. I was pinned in the fighting chair. Nowhere to run. And all I could see was a three-foot spear backed by 350 pounds of fishy mass closing the gap. I was stuck in the chair. Nowhere to go. Time slowed as the fish grew in size as it approached the boat, my impending doom closing in.

I let go of the fishing rod and put my arms up over my head. I closed my eyes and braced for impact.

It sounded like a side of beef running head on into a brick wall at 40 miles per hour.

The fish had closed the 20-foot gap between itself and the boat in just a second or two, falling out of the sky as suddenly as it took off. It smashed into the transom of the boat, its head whipping toward the cabin, the bill coming just inches from my nose. The impact made a tremendous thud that sent the whole boat into a shudder. I was in shock. For a second I wondered if I was dead, the bill slicing into my neck like a razorblade.

My hearing came back. My vision focused. I felt my face to see if my nose, lips and eyes were all in place. I looked at my palms fully expecting to find blood. They were clean. The fish barely missed flying straight into the cockpit. A few more inches of air and it would've landed in my lap.

Who's the pussy now?

An air of silence fell over the crew as we assessed the damage. Brad, check. Pico, check. Parker, check. Quinn, check. All accounted for.

Brad had made the right move at the right time when he decided to let go of the leader. "That fish was still real green," he said to Quinn up in the tower. "It never really made any big jumps before we got it to the leader, man. I felt it start digging and that's when I let go."

Watching a blue marlin leap at the end of a line makes the animal look powerful and majestic, but when a big billfish comes straight at you bill first, it looks downright scary.

"That fish was gnarly!" Quinn screamed. From Quinn's vantage point in the tower, the fish appeared at eye level. It had gotten that much air. Michael Jordan would be proud. "That was the most precise Crazy Ivan I've ever seen!"

The pandemonium that ensued after impact took a few minutes to subside, and nobody noticed the fish floating belly up behind the boat. Once recomposed, I grabbed the rod that was still hooked to the fish and reeled it back toward the boat. We thought the blow had stunned the fish, or knocked it out. Brad grabbed the bill and held the fish beside the hull. Only then did we realize it was definitely a blue marlin. Its pectoral fins were retractable, unlike the black marlin, which has fixed pec fins. But unfortunately, it was a dead blue marlin.

We pulled the fish with the boat for 15 minutes, running water through its gills, performing CPR on the fish. We hoped moving water through its lungs would bring the fish back to life. Some of its coloring reappeared, pushing off the bronze sepia tones that took over the electric blues as life slipped out of its body. We let the fish go, but as we motored away, we could see the marlin floating. The crew decided to retrieve the animal rather than leave it for the sharks. When we pulled the marlin into the boat, Pico noticed something strange sticking out of its back.

The transom of *Intimidator* has a door known as a tuna door, which swings outward so you can pull large fish into the cockpit rather than lifting them up and over the covering boards. There is also a clip and doorstop mounted on the transom that holds the door open and then releases the door when you push the release tab on the clip. When the fish made contact with the boat, this blunt-faced doorstop rammed into the marlin.

The power and momentum of the animal was so great that when it made contact with the blunt, rubber-faced doorstop — the little nub meant to keep the tuna door open became a deadly weapon, severing the fish's spine and rendering the animal motionless.

Another two or three inches and the fish's momentum would have carried it all the way into the cockpit, where it would have likely slapped and kicked us into a befuddled mess of broken fiberglass and crushed bones — a potentially deadly situation. Our wails of excitement could have easily been screams of terror.

A quick push on the throttles kept us all out of harm's way.

"I think everyone on board will remember this day for the rest of their lives," Quinn said. "I know I certainly will."

After the dust settled and the excitement somewhat dwindled to a more controllable roar, I found the lure and held it up in my hands. Written in black letters across the lure's silvery insert were the words "Marlin Punch."

CHAPTER TEN

The One-Eyed Eel

"Have you ever had a girl try to kiss you right after she finishes sucking you off?" Tony Masino asked, sitting behind the wheel of his 46-foot seiner that he'd converted for sport fishing and some light commercial work. We were somewhere in the Gulf of Alaska, motoring between a few of Tony's coveted halibut spots. We'd been at sea for four days. The fish hold was filling up and we were running out of shit to talk about.

"Sure," I said. "They all do that."

"Why?" he asked, dropping his fist onto the top of the steering wheel. "I mean most of us, well, I don't know about you, but we all try at some point to suck our own dick, right? I didn't taste it then and I don't want to taste it now."

"It's a test," I replied. "They want to see if you still think they're pretty. If you still respect them after they just had your dick in their mouth."

Tony shook his head: "I don't get it, Parker. Most of the women who will actually go down on me are not exactly pretty to begin with." He had a point. Tony was a squat guy, not more than five-foot-eight and his once stocky frame had widened over the years. In his twenties and thirties, Tony was a powerhouse. Shoulders like a garbage can. His short-man mentality manifested itself in fairly routine outbursts that gained him a lot of respect on the docks in Seward, Alaska. He'd help any other captain, but if you did something underhanded or fucked with his boat in any way, you'd know about it. No matter how big you were, Tony would find a way to fuck you up. His uppercut broke jaws and hospitalized men who outweighed him by 60 pounds. He'd swing first and ask questions later. A tactic he learned at an early age. His motto: "If you get a chance to take the first punch, don't be a pussy — take it." But you better make it count. No second punches needed.

Now approaching 50 with a gray beard and not much hair on top, Tony didn't fight anymore. He didn't have to. His reputation was intact. He didn't have to take the first shot. He owned these docks, or at least he walked them like he did, and he was my friend.

Tony and I first met on a head boat in Montauk. I was with Daddy and Tony was working as a deckhand for the summer. He was 15 years older than me. I was in my late teens and Tony hooked me up with some weed and snuck me into the local dive bars. I barely looked 18 but Tony got me in, no questions asked. We stayed in touch. A few years after that first meeting, Tony followed his dream and bought a boat in Alaska. He never went back to the Lower 48.

Although an outsider with roots in New York City of all places, Tony earned more than a reputation as an ass-kicker. He quickly rose through the ranks as one of the top charter boats in town. He won the Seward Halibut Derby three years in a row, which pissed off a lot of people. Tony's face smiling proudly in the *Alaska Dispatch News*. And the ornerier the locals got, the more Tony laughed. If he lost, he was a gentleman about it. He'd shake the winning captain's hand and quickly start in with the questions: How deep? Current? Tide? Coordinates? Bait? He had a love-hate relationship with a lot of the other captains in town, but if the shit hit the fan, he'd never leave a fellow mariner. He'd stay with you if your boat was in trouble or bring you fuel if you were adrift and heading toward trouble. You've got to help out if you can. It might be you one day.

"What if the shoe's on the other foot?" shouted a voice from the aft deck of the boat. It was Phil, Tony's mate. "Do you try to kiss the girl after you go down on her?"

"Not necessarily," I said. "I mean chowing the box is just foreplay to a guy. Greasing the wheels. Getting them fired up so you can have sex with them, right? I guess it's the same for some girls, but most of them want to please you. They get off on making you happy. It's not the act of cumming they're after, it's the act of *them* making you cum. It's not even about getting laid."

"You're an idiot, Parker," Tony said. "Some women just want to get laid. If they didn't, we'd never get any."

"I like eating out chicks," Phil said. "Making 'em wiggle. That's how I got my nickname."

"What nickname?" Tony asked.

"Philacious Phil."

Tony and I looked at each other, half smiling.

"Like fallacious?" I asked.

"Yeah, man. That's the technical term for eating out a girl," Phil said.

Tony and I both laughed out loud.

"I don't think so, Philacious Phil," I said in between laughs that boiled up from my gut. "Fallacious is a fallacy. Like literally, it means fallacy ... fake."

Phil didn't much like being laughed at. He stood up from the bait-cutting table and stared me down.

"What's so funny about that, Parker?" he said with a sneer that made me take a hard swallow. He was holding a knife and his work bibs were covered in blood. He could star in a horror flick.

Phil had the exact opposite body shape of Tony. He was a giant, measuring exactly six feet, 10 inches. And I know this only because we went to an outdoor concert that summer, and rather than answer the question a hundred times, he took black shoe polish and had someone write 6'10" on his bare back. Whenever someone began to ask, "Hey man, how tall ..." Phil would turn around and show them the signage. I feel badly for whoever sat behind him at that concert. He was at least a full head taller than any other man I knew.

Being so large may act as a strength in some arenas like a basketball court or when painting a room with high ceilings, but trying to get around a boat isn't exactly easy for big men. Phil bumped his head at least 29 times a day, and he had to fold his body up like origami just to take a shit in the boat's head, his knees up by his ears and his head pinned sideways against the low ceiling. I once walked in on him by accident (the lock was busted) and he asked me to help him wipe. He said it was nearly impossible to get the right angle. I kindly refused, horrified at the thought.

Most tall guys are clumsy, which is only amplified when they are placed on a pitching boat. Not Phil. He had the dexterity of a man two feet shorter than him. And he was fast. He could hook a bait and get it in the water on one side of the boat and in a flash be on the other side, gaffing a monster halibut and hauling it over the rail like it was a sand dab. He was quite possibly the strongest human being I'd ever met. I watched in awe as he'd pull 200-pound fish up and over the side of the boat like he was flipping pancakes.

Big halibut are usually not the first fish to show up when fishing the bottom. You must cull through some chickens before the big ones appear. The fish seemingly get bigger with every bite. And the more small fish you catch, the more attention you begin to get from the giants. Keep fishing, keep chumming and you may eventually land a triple-digit fish weighing upward of 300 pounds. Catching barn doors doesn't often happen by accident. You must put in your time, find your spots and record the locations. A captain's numbers, the coordinates of his best spots, are his most valuable asset.

When the bite peaks, you often get multiple hookups. A good thing, especially when fishing for poundage. And with Phil's long wingspan he could stretch across the deck like an octopus. He'd gaff a fish on the port side with one hand and grab a rod amidship with his other. He never stopped moving. It was a trait he picked up as a cage fighter. No shit. For a brief period, Phil was into motorcycles and rode with a few different biker gangs. He was a good enforcer, and one notorious gang that I'm a little afraid to mention had decided to sanction him as a cage fighter after one of their members witnessed Phil take on four guys in a bar fight. He put all four men in the hospital, never taking a punch, laughing the entire time. I certainly didn't want to end up like one of those four guys. I stopped laughing and Tony segued the conversation back to fellatio or masturbation — I don't really remember.

I made my way to the bait table and started to chop some herring and pack them into brown lunch bags, which Tony calls chum bombs. To make a chum bomb you fill a bag about one-third full with bait chunks and cinch the paper down, twisting it with your hands so it looks like an upside-down lollipop. We had a designated bomb rod to drop the bits of bait down into the deep. We'd use a rubber band to attach the bomb to the fishing line and drop it down into the deep with a 10-ounce lead weight. Once the bomb was where we wanted it, a good yank on the rod ripped the bag open, releasing the chum. It worked great. But making chum bombs was a dirty, somewhat thoughtless job. I wore plastic gloves to protect my hands from the smell and the chill of the still-frozen herring. Cutting bait becomes hypnotic after a while. Line up three herrings, cut the tail, make two or three more cuts along the body, and then with the last swipe of the knife remove the head. Slide the cut bait down the table into a pile. Line up three more herring. Repeat. The brain wanders. You may whistle. Songs inevitably get stuck in your internal stereo.

I was humming along to a Led Zeppelin tune in my head when the record scratched. I felt a bear paw swipe at me from the back, knocking off my hat.

"What the fuck, man?" I said, turning to find Philacious Phil with a distressed look on his face.

"Parker, I'm hurt bad. Real bad," he said. A shot of fear jolted through me. Those are words no one likes to hear anywhere, but hurting yourself at sea is life-threatening.

"What? What happened?!"

Phil's face was white. He looked seasick or something. His head slowly moved down, his gaze rolling toward his feet. I followed the gaze and saw blood. His rubber bibs had a small tear around his groin and brownish-red blood was smeared everywhere. The crimson liquid ran from the area of his navel to the foot of his right leg. But it wasn't the blood that was rattling me. I couldn't quite place the origin of the animal latched onto Phil, with a hook on the other end. Was it a conger eel? Conger eels are black. It wasn't black. Some kind of elongated hake? I leaned a bit closer. Oh, good lord, I thought, he's somehow hooked his penis. Is that his penis? My God, how in the world ... It's the size of a vacuum hose. Like a long, winding hose used on a Shop-Vac.

"Help me, man!" he yelled. "Get it out!"

"Get what out?" I yelled back at him.

Phil's giant prick was hooked by a 12/0 circle hook that ran clear through the head of his unit, the point of the hook barely sticking out one side and the shank or straight side of the hook lying flat against the other. To get this hook out I was going to have to push the barb fully out of his penis, clip the barb off and pull the hook back through the wound from the opposite direction.

"Tony, we have to go in!" I hollered.

"What the fuck are you talking about?" Tony said. "We've only caught half of our quota."

"Phil's hurt!"

"How bad? Is he going to die?"

"I don't know, man, but I might," I said.

"What? Just deal with it, Parker, please."

"How in the fuck did you do this?" I asked Phil.

"I don't know, man. A fish spit the hook and the line was tight and the hook just caught me there."

I put down the bait knife and dropped to my knees to get a closer look, but Phil is so fucking tall I probably could've gotten the job done from my feet. I was eye to eye with the beast. Blood was everywhere, making it difficult to assess the severity of the injury.

"Can you wash it off?" I asked.

"Just get it out, man! Please!" Phil yelled, wincing on each breath.

I slowly lifted my gloved left hand up and was about to grab his knob, which looked like the handle of a baseball bat. This would mark a first in my life. I was certainly no medic. I'd never come so close to another man's private parts. Maybe I could tell stories in the bar about it one day, I thought to myself. "Remember that time I unhooked your giant cock, Phil?"

My arm, however, turned to stone. I tried to open my fingers but they were balled into a tight fist. The forces inside me were

151

colliding like a train wreck. I wanted to help but something deep down in my psyche was putting up a wall. It wasn't the gore. I've seen plenty of blood in my day. I've been nipples deep inside of a giant tuna, pulling out the animal's innards and loving it. I've gutted the most foul-smelling fowl without even gagging. But not this. I wasn't prepared for this.

My vision slowly started to blur from the outside edges, my stomach inside out. The periphery began to go black. I tried to fight it off and shook my head wildly, but the darkness flew in from each side of my sight like two curtains closing. Thunk.

"Parker, wake up! Parker!" It was Tony's voice. The blood rushed back to my head. I opened my eyes and saw Tony's smiling face. He smacked me hard on the cheek. "You all right, man?"

"Where's Phil?" I asked. "Is he okay?"

"I'm right here, you dumbass," Phil said.

I was sitting on the deck of the boat, my back propped up against the bait table. The eel was still flying about, but Phil was no longer in pain. He was laughing.

"Watch this," Phil said as he easily slid the hook out of his penis, which he had left out of his pants for his amusement or Tony's, I'm not sure.

The sight of the hook sliding out made me nauseous and my vision began to blur again until Tony smacked me for the second time.

"Is that some sort of circus trick?" I asked.

"He got you," Tony said. "He's done it to all of us."

"I've got a penis stud, man," Phil said. "Chicks love it. When I get bored on the boat I file the barb down on a circle hook and shove it through my cock just to fuck with people." Phil could hardly contain his joy at my demise. "I've never had anyone pass out like that though."

I looked at Tony, his head cocked back, laughter loudly booming out of him. Phil was on one knee now, cleaning himself off with a hose. The tip of his penis touching the deck of the boat.

"I want to go home," I said.

CHAPTER ELEVEN

The Mother's Day Hatch

"One of these days, when you're older, I will take you."

I heard that phrase a lot. Every time I saw Daddy putting together his fishing gear in the corner of our basement, rod tubes, reels, tackle and a few pieces of clothing, I would pester him about taking me. I didn't care where he was going. I wanted that alone time with him. I craved it like a second cup of coffee. I knew he was heading off to some magical place. A mountain stream. A forgotten patch of mangroves south of the Florida Everglades. The less he told me about the place he was headed, the more I wanted to tag along. My mind's eye painting brilliant pictures of clear waters, massive fish and unspoken adventures in tricked-out vessels with wild, cowboy-like guides who never backed down from a fish fight.

"Please, Daddy. I'll be good. I swear."

He'd smile. Tussle my hair.

"In a few years, Parker. I promise."

When he passed, I began going to all of the places he had meant to take me to. Places I knew he wanted me to experience. Top of that list was Montana, fly-fishing for trout in wide rivers under a banner of tall peaks and a shaggy landscape.

Daddy was not a purist fly-fisherman, nor am I, but a calling to the mountains lived in his heart. He would dream of trout streams. He needed the sound of a running river to clear his head. The never-ending rhythm of moving water to chase away the demons of business and the demands of life. He longed for cold mornings that forced you into activity to warm the blood. Fog hovering over the river valley and hiding the peaks until the sun broke through, which it never did on some days. An inspired landscape. A place where you saw your breath in the air and welcomed it.

He'd return home with stories that kept me up for hours,

sometimes days. I couldn't stop my mind from exploring the pictures he painted with his soft voice, sitting on the edge of the bed. His rough hands cupping my cheek. His thumb smoothing down the hair along my temples. I couldn't sleep knowing there was a place like Montana out there in the world waiting for me. Trout as thick as fence posts, gorging on insects. These visions haunted me for days until I too succumbed to the world we live in. School. Girls. Sports. They'd all eventually take over and I'd cascade into my privileged life until Daddy would tell me a story about the river and our shared passion would come alive in me once again.

The soft orange glow of the nightlight next to my bed projected a big shadow of him onto the ceiling, making him look more like a god than a man.

"Have I ever told you about the time Willy and I fished the Mother's Day hatch?" he asked. Willy was Daddy's most trusted employee and his best friend. A man I knew my entire life. I called him Uncle Willy.

"No," I said. "What's a hatch?"

"There are all of these insects that live in the rivers and streams. Mayflies, stoneflies and caddisflies. At a certain time of year, when the temperature is just right and the angle of the sun in the sky sits at this perfect spot, the bugs begin to hatch."

"In the river?" I asked.

"Yes, well sort of. They rise up in the water and by the time they hit the surface of the river, their wings unfurl and they fly off." He used his hands to mimic the erratic movements of a freshly hatched bug.

I imagined bugs shooting out of the river like rockets launched from a submarine.

"The trout go into a feeding frenzy during the hatch. The river comes alive," he said. "The caddis hatch in Montana usually happens around Mother's Day. And since I never really knew my mother, I usually have that day off," he said, pausing to look at me, smiling. "Me and your Uncle Willy, we got wind of this Mother's Day hatch and we went to the mountains. We got lucky, Parker, and arrived right at the peak of the hatch. It was amazing."

"Wow," I said. "Are the fish big?"

"Some of them, and they're very aggressive because it's one of the first hatches of the season. It's a lot of fun. One of these days, when you're older, I'll take you. Now try to get some rest."

Yeah, right.

Birth of the Caddis

The caddis lives most of its life below the surface, clinging to the slippery stones and soft, leaf-strewn bottom of mountain streams and rivers. These waters are cold, rich in oxygen and ripe for growth — if you can survive.

Each spring, as snow begins to melt, the rivers swell. Rushing waters with enough power to topple boulders the size of a small car surge against the tiny caddis larvae. Roughly the length of a thumbnail, the larvae is vulnerable, but this creature perseveres. Not out of sheer will but out of ingenuity — a form of evolution that hermit crabs seem to have taught them or learned from.

The head, gills and legs of the larval caddisfly are fairly well protected by a layer of armor-like exoskeleton called chitin. The lower body, however, is not so lucky, and its ivory-colored flesh is exposed to hungry trout. The caddis larvae sticks out from the bottom of the river, appearing much like a white bulbous grub. To ward off predators and survive in the hurricane-force current, the caddis uses its natural surroundings to build a casing. Sometimes they use sticks to construct a log cabin in the shape of a small tube, like a hollow straw that they slide into and cruise around with. Other larvae seek out perfectly suited pebbles and create insect mansions like master bricklayers. They bind together the materials they collect into a mini tunnel with a sticky substance akin to a spider's silky web.

The caddis begins with leaves, sticks and bark to provide camouflage and protection. As it grows the insect may move onto more substantial matter like pebbles or better yet, find a vacant home left on the river bottom by one of its brethren. The caddis adheres one tiny boulder at a time, layer by layer, rock by rock, to create a home that provides ballast to fight against the push of moving water and protection from the barrage of hungry fish.

The caddis brushes the surface of the bricks with the homemade glue that it secretes from a gland under its chin. The viscid silk acts like double-sided tape to seal the tiny rocks in place. This caddis adhesive is magical stuff. It stays sticky underwater. It can also stretch so the caddis can pull its rocky home over bumpy terrain without the entire structure falling apart. And the mortar snaps back slowly. There are no quick, jerky movements, which keeps the larvae inside safe and protected. If you've ever been whacked by a sapling pulled forward by someone ahead of you on the trail, you can grasp why it's important for the caddis adhesive to have a slow snapback. DuPont or 3M would love to know how the caddis creates this waterproof, stretchable glue, but no engineer is quite as deft as Mother Nature.

As the larvae matures to the pupae stage, it seals itself up in the case it made from pebbles and settles in for a bit of a nap, resting on the bottom of the river, listening to the constant flush of cold water as its body metamorphosizes. After a month or so in the casing, a nitrogen bubble begins to form. This gas pulls the once bottom-dwelling case into the fast-moving river water. Feeling the rush of moving current, the caddis eagerly carves out an escape hatch, instinctively knowing what is coming next. The gas expands and the insect rises higher in the water column. The cocoon it created begins to split open. The insect's legs work their way to the crack, opening the crevice and pushing back the pupae skin. The caddis is about to hatch. It wiggles itself out head-first like a newborn with six legs. As the caddis hits the surface of the river, the wings emerge. It's now a fully formed, flying insect. The caddis pumps its wings rapidly to clear them of fluid before taking to the air with a soft, feathery, erratic motion, bumbling about like a drunk moth. The magical moment of the hatching caddis triggers a melee of gorging fish on the surface. Hungry trout leap out of the water in hot pursuit of the newly formed insects. Many deaths ensue. A caddis massacre. The only mission left for the surviving caddis is to lay eggs and thus begin the cycle anew.

On the Madison

Uncle Willy put his hand on my left shoulder. We were stepping down from the drift boat to the crunchy gravel of the river bottom. I noticed the many large freckles on his forearm. He was getting old. His once powerful hands were diminished, with long, skinny fingers that almost had a dainty quality to them. But there is nothing dainty about Uncle Willy. I'd known this man my entire life, from the first time I opened my eyes. Willy rode shotgun with Daddy on some of the largest business transactions in the history of their company. They traveled the world, working deals across America, as well as Mexico, Central America and Asia. These two guys never went to college, but they knew how to work hard. They put in long days and even longer years. They also knew how to have fun. They fished. They hunted. They caroused. Daddy and Willy could work from seven in the morning to seven in the evening, go fishing till 10 or 11 p.m., hit the bar, get home at four a.m., sleep for two hours, get up, brush their teeth and head back to the office. They loved every second of it. Making more money than they ever knew they were capable of, and logging adventures from land and sea.

With Daddy gone, Willy helped broker the deal to sell the company to the employees. Pushing 67, he had pulled back on the throttles. He semiretired and took on a smaller role, sitting on the board of directors but not engaging in the day-to-day operations or sales that he had masterfully navigated for three-plus decades.

"I want to do something before we catch any more," he said to me, caddis bouncing around his head. He reached into the chest pocket of his waders and produced an old pill case.

"You taking something?" I asked.

"No," he said, "and even if I was I wouldn't offer you any."

I smiled. He knows me well.

"These are some of your daddy's ashes. We made a deal a long time ago, he and I. Whoever went first had to place the other one in five special spots. This is one of them."

Willy looked down at the pill case in his once powerful hands and sighed. He gripped the cap and attempted to open it. "Stupid fucking thing," he said. "You probably think this is funny, don't you, Joe?"

He handed me the bottle: "Give an old man a hand, Parker, will ya?"

I opened the pill bottle and looked at Willy, our eyes swelling with tears, our throats knotting uncomfortably.

"Go ahead," he said.

I took a couple of steps into the river.

"I finally got here, Daddy. With you," I said softly and poured the contents into the moving waters. The ashes fell slowly, some of them catching on the wind and swirling into small tornadoes as the breeze blew downriver. The ashes that settled on the surface of the river disappeared instantly. I closed my eyes and listened to the water rushing over my boots. I could hear Daddy and Willy telling fishing stories. I could see Daddy's face as he piloted *Long Gone* on the tuna grounds. Feeling at ease, I took a deep breath of the cool Montana air.

A swift push on my back abruptly interrupted my reflective moment, toppling me over onto my hands and knees in the cold water.

"Wake up, son!" he yelled.

"Fuck, that's cold," I said from my knees, my bare hands fully emerged in the 50-degree water. The cuffs of my sweater dripping wet.

"Look there," he said, pointing to the shoreline on the opposite side of the river where a handful of trout were sipping caddis off the surface. "Let's walk downstream a bit so the fish don't notice us and move toward the center of the river. From there we can work a few flies right along that shore. You catch my drift?"

"Good one, Uncle Willy," I said, shaking my head and wiping my wet hands on my sweater. "I'll follow your lead."

The Madison River runs from Yellowstone National Park to the Missouri River. The river is broken into sections, segmented by dams and lakes. Portions of the river move swiftly and foam with

Class IV rapids. Kayakers love these lumpy stretches where the river becomes a frenetic highway, but fishermen do not. Those who like to loft flies at hungry trout prefer the gentle waters that run through the gorgeous Madison Valley. Every direction you gaze offers unmolested views of jagged mountains and enough open space to quiet the storms inside a man's head. The river is a constantly changing maze of riffles and pools to investigate with dry flies, streamers and nymphs.

I am by no means a fly-fishing dogmatist, but I appreciate the sport. I love the feeling of a light fly rod in my hands. I appreciate the skinny, whippy rods for what they are, simple tools that do their job well. Once made from natural materials like hickory or bamboo, fly rods are now built using space-age technologies. Feather light with enough flex in the tip to zing a near weightless fly to the far corner of a river, the rods can cost a small fortune, but they're meticulously crafted to pull their weight. And if you take care of your gear, it may outlive you.

The rods have morphed from organic materials to fiberglass and graphite, but a handful of anglers are reverting to the homemade cane poles of yesteryear. That's because fly anglers love to make things as hard as possible. To make fishing an art form. To inspire the soul. A spinning reel may get the job done more efficiently, with great ease and little cost, but what's the fun in that? You could run out and buy a little rooster tail and catch trout all day on a spinner, but it's much more fulfilling to see a fish suck down a miniscule dry fly that you tied yourself using bucktail and chicken feathers.

Granted, I am not opposed to fishing with spinning rods or heavy conventional gear when conditions or the chosen target dictates, but if I'm going after trout, the only weapon I would ever use is a fly rod.

There is something very Zen about standing in a moving river on a wide-open plain capped with peaks so tall that trees can't grow on their summits. You may spy a bear or moose walking by. Herds of elk grazing in the distance. This landscape inspires me. It's my church. It sets my mind free. That's trout fishing, to me. No other form of fishing immerses you so completely into the fish's habitat. I think that's how Daddy felt too, even though Uncle Willy said he was no good at fly-fishing.

Daddy loved casting a fly rod. He took casting lessons from some of the greatest anglers in the sport and could place a fly anywhere he wanted. "The trick," Daddy would say, "is to not get upset if you make a bad cast and hang up on a tree branch or lose your tippet. If you let your failures get the most of you, you'll never recover. You'll never be able to make that perfect cast when it really matters. Laugh it off and bring plenty of flies because getting hung up happens to everyone."

Trout anglers often fish from a drift boat. You can cover much more ground this way, with one man working the oars to keep the boat in position for a couple of anglers to make cast after cast. Daddy liked to walk the river. To take his time and work his way into the moving water when he found fish.

"I've always liked being able to carry everything I need to go fishing right here in my vest," Daddy said as I watched him pack his gear before one of his trips. "But I keep backups of everything in the truck."

Losing flies and tying many knots over the course of a day's fishing is actually part of the fun. At times, you may feel rushed to get back in the game, but that's when you need to slow down. Read the river. Evaluate the movement of the water. Learn about the insects around you and try to understand the behavior of the fish. Take a step back. Think like a fish. Turn the other shit off.

The five-weight fly rod in my hand for this trip actually belonged to Daddy. I don't know when or where he picked it up, but I grabbed it out of the pile of gear that still sits in the basement of his house, which I have yet to change. The custom rod is a four-piece, all black with his name handwritten in golden marker under the protection of several coats of smooth epoxy: "Joe McPhee, 5 Wt." I packed his waders for this trip too. While I may never be able to fill his shoes in many ways, Daddy's waders fit me quite nicely. I don't have his belly yet, but I stand just an inch or two shorter than he did. A quick adjustment on the suspenders and a new wading belt were all I needed.

I took another few steps into the river, literally standing in my father's shoes in one of his most treasured fishing spots. I had not felt this close to him since his passing. My feet moved slowly, quietly shuffling over the slippery rocks. My eyes focused on a pair of fish in a pool on the far side of the river.

"Parker, do you have an elk-hair caddis on?" Willy whispered. He was standing about three feet upriver, his eyes transfixed on the same section of water I was about to cast toward.

I nodded 'yes.'

"Throw it upriver, as close to the shore as you can."

I pulled some fly line off the reel and let it rest in the water. I made a few false casts to build up my momentum. I reminded myself that I wasn't tarpon fishing. I'm more accustomed to longer casts, heavier gear and vicious strike-sets to place that hook firmly in the bony mouth of a tarpon. If I were to strip-set a trout, I'd yank the small fly right out of its grasp. To set the hook here, you must lift the rod tip at precisely the right moment when the fly is in the fish's mouth. It may sound simple, but it's not.

My first cast fell a good two feet shy of the shoreline but I let it drift downriver, mending the line so the fly would look as natural as possible and not drag against the current. No takers. I walked upstream a couple of more steps. I flicked the fly behind me to load the rod with energy, which is then transferred forward to sling the fly out ahead of you. I made three or four false casts, keeping the fly in the air while I pulled more line off the reel and prepared to make a longer cast.

The wind had died down and clouds were beginning to form but my vision remained locked on the opposite side of the river. The second cast was a bit closer to the shoreline, but the fly did not land properly. Rather than unfurl smoothly, the line sort of plopped down in a ball with too much slack in the water. I picked the fly up with the rod and began to make more false casts. That's when I saw my fish. It was two feet long with its nose pinned against the current. The trout hung a foot behind a large boulder just askew of midstream. I adjusted my cast while the fly was in the air and aimed for the section of river in front of the rock. The fly dropped down softly. I flicked the tip of the rod to adjust the line in the water and set the drift. I watched the grayish-brown fly float downstream in the current. The fly wasn't large, maybe the size of a dime. It fell over the boulder silently and disappeared.

"There he is!" Willy exclaimed.

I resisted the urge to set the hook by yanking on the line as I do when targeting tarpon. I lifted the rod tip high with my right hand and held the fly line with my left until I felt the line come tight.

"Goddamn, that trout sucked you dry, Parker!" Willy said, hooting and hollering like a frat boy.

The fish launched itself, cartwheeling across the cascading river. A gorgeous rainbow trout with speckled sides and a swath of pink flesh running down its lateral line, giving way to a reddish, blushing cheek. I held the rod tip high and felt the cool, wet fly line shoot through my fingers as the fish flew downstream. I stepped downriver awkwardly, keeping the rod high in the air and trying not to fall on my face as I watched the fish and not where I was stepping. The fish kept running down-current. My hands were shaking from the adrenaline, or maybe the cold water. The trout was as fast as a bonefish. It leapt like a sailfish. I had no idea how I would catch it. The fly line was long gone in what felt like a millisecond and I was into the backing on the fly reel. I adjusted my hold on the cork grip so I could better handle the rod as the fish ran for rocks and coverage, darting back and forth across the river.

"Tip up," Willy said. "Keep the tip up!"

I felt Daddy there with me. Telling me to slow down. To be calm. To appreciate the moment. The fish was not done jumping, leaping two feet in the air and flipping backward. I seized every opportunity to gain line, but I didn't rush it. When the fish wanted to run, I let him. When I could crank line back on, I turned the small reel handle as fast as I could. I admired the animal's moves. I didn't want the fight to end, but I also knew it wouldn't last forever and if I made a mistake, the tippet would break. The fish would sneak away. The memory would be altered. A catch lost. I didn't want that to happen.

The trout's bright pinks and speckled sides blazed through the waist-deep water like a submerged street light. The fish was tiring. The line began to come in easier. The rainbow was giving up, but gaining the last few yards of line was the toughest of the fight. I lifted the rod high above me and pulled the rod tip back past my head so I could grab the tippet with my left hand. I knew the added pressure of me holding the line in my hand may break the tippet, but I went for it anyway. I reached around to the back of my vest for my net, but it wasn't there. How the hell did I forget a net? My one hope was to grab the fish.

"Don't grab the fish! I have a net," Willy hollered as he worked his way toward me. I didn't have the patience to wait for him. I feared this may be my only chance to land this trout.

I grasped the tippet with my left hand and slid the rod under my right arm so I could use both hands to scoop up the fish. The trout turned slightly onto its side, as if it wanted me to give it a hug. I gently put my hands around the beautiful animal. The fish was in my cold, shaking hands.

"Man, you sure are lucky," Willy said, standing next to me with his landing net in his hand.

I don't know if the fish was really 24 inches, but that's what Uncle Willy called it. I rubbed my hands under the trout's smooth belly and lifted it out of the water briefly so Uncle Willy could capture the moment on his cell phone.

I've had only a few hand-shaking moments in my life, where the energy and excitement is too much for your body to contain and you begin to shake … with joy. This was one of those moments.

The memory floodgates opened as I admired the beauty of this creature and its environment. I thought about fishing with Daddy and Jensi. I thought about the boats we had run. The places we'd gone. The teenage angst and anger in my heart was slipping away. I forgave my father for missing parts of my life that I felt were important. Forgotten baseball games or graduations. He gave me so much. He gave me this memory, and many others. He taught me how to love and appreciate the beauty of our oceans and rivers. Between us, fishing had become a common language. It brought us together and let us forge unthinkable adventures. Fishing is not about catching the biggest fish to hang on your wall; it's about celebrating time with people you enjoy. Catching a fish is a gift.

This life that he built for me is a gift.

I looked down at the colorful trout one last time, holding it in the water and turning it in my hands to see its pink and blue and green flesh sparkle in the daylight. I went to remove the fly, but it had already fallen out. The fish must've hardly been hooked. It was a miracle that I had caught the trout at all.

"Thank you, Daddy," I said, and let it swim away.

EPILOGUE

I am not Parker McPhee.

My life has been blessed in many ways and I have been fortunate to fish the world's oceans with incredible captains and characters, but I am not Parker. These are not my stories; these are Parker's stories. With that said, this book would've never been possible had I not met and fished with captains like Andy Mezirow of Seward, Alaska; Tim Richardson of Gold Coast, Australia; Brad Philipps of Guatemala by way of South Africa; Josh Temple of Tofino, British Columbia; John Gregory of Kerikeri, New Zealand, and many others who have welcomed me on their boat and taken me fishing. To all of the captains and guides who have become my friends, I thank you.

When I was 11, I asked my father for a typewriter. It seemed like a strange gift for a young boy when most others wanted G.I. Joe action figures, but he obliged. I knew that I wanted to be a writer. I dreamt of writing crime novels and stories of mafia families, and I started many tales in those genres, but I never finished them. Mostly because I didn't know what the hell I was talking about. But the dream of writing a book persisted. It just took me a long time to figure out what to write.

In 2012, I was invited on a press trip to fish for tarpon, bonefish and permit in Cuba. Jim Klug of Yellow Dog Fly Fishing Adventures organized the trip, and I was somehow one of a dozen journalists invited. I believe it was the urging of Tom Bie, editor of *The Drake*, who suggested Jim invite me. Perhaps they wanted a conventional angler's take on the incredible waters that make up the Jardines de la Reina. Thanks, Tom. And thank you, Jim.

It was on this trip to Cuba that the genesis of *Sucked Dry* began to form. As the lone lure fisherman in a gaggle of fly guys, I was asked a lot of questions. Where's the best place to find billfish? How can you catch a 500-pound fish? These questions led to longer tales about big fish and the hijinks often associated with offshore anglers. We listened to music, threw back cervezas on *La Tortuga*, the mothership we were staying on, and we laughed our asses off.

I like to tell stories, especially funny ones, so I kept on going. The other writers did the same. We laughed a lot, but one writer, Chris Santella, author of *Fifty Places to Fly Fish Before You Die*, kept encouraging me to write these funny fishing stories down. "Fishing isn't just about catching fish," he said. "It's about the adventure. The take. The experience." Those words hung with me, and when I got home I began writing. Chris, I can't thank you enough. I would've never thought of weaving these tales into a book if it weren't for your kind words.

But a funny thing happened as I plugged along on this book: I had a son. Then I had a second son. When my boys entered the picture, I began reflecting on my own upbringing. I thought about the time fishing with my father on his boats. How much he loved the ocean. How the days we spent fishing together shaped me into the man I became. We bonded more on those boats than we ever did on land. That's part of fishing too. Those reflections impacted *Sucked Dry*, hopefully for the better, and to my father, Mark Levine, I owe you a very special thank you. As a father, I now know how hard you worked to provide for us. I understand why your time on the water was so important. Thanks for everything you did for me and the family.

Finally, I feel a bit remiss about the lack of female characters in this book. Throughout my life I have been greatly influenced by strong women. My grandmother, my mother, my sister, my wife. Thank you all for everything you've taught me, for your love and your support.

I hope you've enjoyed *Sucked Dry*. There are a few more Parker McPhee stories that I plan to tell, so stay tuned. And if you'd like to follow along on my adventures, visit my blog at thestruggleisreel.com.

ABOUT THE AUTHOR

Charlie Levine was born and raised in Connecticut, where he developed a love of fishing and boating. After graduating from Western State Colorado University with a degree in English and journalism, he briefly worked in the newspaper industry. Writing about death, murder and mayhem wasn't his bag, so he made a switch and began to write about subjects he was passionate about, namely the outdoors, adventure and food. He has written hundreds of articles for fishing and travel publications. He currently lives in Central Florida with his wife, Diane, and sons, Maxon and Cooper.

Made in the USA
Lexington, KY
13 June 2018